YOUTH • WORK • PRESS

Published by

17-23 Albion Street, Leciester LE1 6GD.
Tel: 0116.285.3700. Fax: 0116.285.3777.
E-Mail: nya@nya.org.uk
Internet: http://www.nya.org.uk

ISBN 0 86155 250 4

£12.95

Editor/Designer: Denise Duncan
Illustrations: Sebastian Buccheri

YOUTH • WORK • PRESS
is the publishing imprint of the National Youth Agency

PREFACE

Young people's life chances depend on many factors. Some of these - from global economics to genetic inheritance - are well beyond the capacity of youth workers to affect. But, in some key areas, we can make a very important impact. None of these is more important than the quality of relationships that a young person is able to build with those around them - whether it be their family, their boyfriend or girlfriend, their peer group, those in authority or others in the wider community.

All young people will benefit from the opportunity to rehearse sensitive issues, to test out their feelings and their values, to stretch their imagination and their capacity for empathy. Providing a supportive and developmental structure for such opportunities is an important task for youth workers and others who work with young people, not least personal advisers within the Connexions Service. Such work enhances the ability to fulfil potential in the fields of learning and employment, but perhaps more importantly it can help young people to be happy.

Tom Wylie
Chief Executive
National Youth Agency

CONTENTS

CONTRIBUTORS

With many thanks to

Zoey Caldwell, Ann McKay, Ingrid Davies, Ben Carr and Lorraine Clark (Young Citizens Project, North), Charlotte Rogers, Jeanette Williams (Young Citizens Project, South), Anie Twigg (Hertfordshire Careers Service Ltd), Deborah Morgan (Youth Offending Team, North Herts), Gillian Porter (QE11), Tony Hunt (HCC Learning Services), Catherine Ward (Dunstable Youth Offending Team), Martin Cooke, Mary Westgate and Carol Hawkes (HCC Youth Service), David Moses, Deborah Mulroney (HCC Education Department), Jani Noakes (HCC Education Welfare Services) and Mike Smith (HCC Education Development Officer).

Thanks also to any youth workers not mentioned who have been a part of the projects that are referred to.

ABOUT THE AUTHOR

Vanessa Rogers is a qualified youth worker with a masters degree in Community Education and ten years experience within Hertfordshire Youth Service both at practitioner and management levels. She has gained extensive experience managing a large youth centre, developing detached projects and working directly with young people in urban and rural parts of the county. Currently employed within the Hertfordshire Youth Justice service, Vanessa uses her skills to provide a youth work approach by presenting preventative solutions for young people at risk of offending or disaffection. She is also the author of *Have you ever ...?* a resource handbook for detached youth workers also published by the National Youth Agency.

SETTING UP THE GROUP

Encouraging young people to talk about sensitive issues and open up about their feelings for themselves and their relationships places a huge responsibility on youth workers to 'get it right'. The success of some of these groupwork activities depends upon creating a safe and supportive environment in which the young people can work.

THE GROUP

Before you start consider the reasons why you are setting up the group. The answer to this will determine your target group to invite or encourage to participate. For groupwork that aims to look at personal issues, such as relationships, a smaller group of about eight young people works well. You can decide if the group is to be mixed gender, but in my experience young men and women often prefer to talk about love, sex and friendship in single-sex groups. The issues that you decide to cover will also need to be age appropriate and take into account individual learning styles and needs.

ENVIRONMENT

Try and create a relaxing environment in which to hold the sessions. Decide if the group is to be a closed group or a drop in and ensure that other users of the building are aware of this and respect it. Set the room up in advance so that there is no last minute shuffling about as you rush around trying to secure all the comfy chairs in the youth centre! Circles work well as everyone can see each other and encourage conversation.

Decide if the group is to be a closed group or a drop in and ensure that other users of the building are aware of this and respect it.

BOUNDARIES

Make sure that you are straight with the young people from the first session. Ensure that both you and they are aware of the boundaries that you have set for the group and also your legal duty regarding child protection issues. One way of explaining this to the young people is to state that the relationship they have with you and the group is confidential, unless they disclose to you that they are either at risk of being harmed or of harming someone else. Make sure that they know that you will then have a duty to act upon the information they give. The young people then have a choice of how much they wish to share.

GROUNDRULES

The young people will need to work together to produce a contract that they are all happy to work with. However, as the issues you are hoping to explore with the group can be extremely sensitive make sure that confidentiality and the need to respect each others' points of view and experiences are fully considered.

RESPECT

It is important that the group becomes a place that nurtures and celebrates difference. Young people should be encouraged and supported in respecting differences within the group, such as sexuality, gender, disability or race. The group needs to accept that each of them will bring their own experiences of love, family, friendship and sexual relationships and that no single viewpoint is necessarily right or representative of everyone's opinion.

PARTICIPATION

Encourage all members of the group to take part. It is often easier for quieter members to opt out of sessions rather than challenge the authority of more assertive young people. This can result in a few strong characters dominating the whole group and working through their own issues without thought to anyone else.

EVALUATION

The process by which you plan to evaluate the success of the group will need to be decided at the planning stage. When you agree your aims for each session, your evaluation methods should show whether these were met or missed completely! Make sure that you involve the young people in the evaluation process so that they can assess their own learning and experiences as well as providing excellent feedback for you.

CONSENT FORMS

If you plan to engage young people in activities that need a risk assessment, or that will involve potentially contentious issues, you should always try and obtain parental/carers consent. If the young people are over 18 they can give this themselves. If not we have devised a consent form that explains clearly what you are planning to cover. This allows parents, carers and young people to make informed choices about whether they want to take part. For some young people you will need to consider their cultural or religious background and decide if the work you are hoping to do will meet their needs. If not, consult with them to plan additional work that meets these too.

Finally, if there is an accident or a problem later you have the information to hand to support the young people. It can be easily altered to suit most events and activities.

AIM
To provide information about the session you have planned with young people.

YOU WILL NEED
- A copy for each group member

HOW TO DO IT
Prepare the consent forms. The emergency number given for contacting the group during the session can be your mobile and/or the youth office.

Hand out copies of the consent form at least a week before you want the project or activity to start. Examples when you might need consent forms are sessions around sexual health, contraception or drugs/alcohol misuse.

Explain to the young people that you need them to show the form to whoever has responsibility for them, to get it signed and return it before the session starts next week.

Either you or your co-worker should assume responsibility for holding these for the duration of the session. If you plan a block of sessions for a project, put all the dates and details on the consent form, so it only has to go home once for signing.

After the project the consent forms can be filed with your evaluation sheets.

Consent Form

Project/Club name ....

Outline of session ....

Date..

Time..

Until..

I give consent for ....(name of young person) to be allowed to take part in this session and to participate in the activities involved.

Signature (Parent or Guardian) ....

Date..

Address and telephone number ....

....

....

Medical conditions

It is really important that we should know of any pre-existing medical condition (for example, asthma, diabetes, heart trouble), which may require treatment and/or any condition which may affect participation in any activity.

He/she suffers from ....which may require treatment.

Please list known allergies to drugs or other medication, e.g. antibiotics and plasters.....

....

If known, date of last immunisation against tetanus...

National Health Service Medical Card Number ....

Is there any other information which you believe we should know? ....

....

Do you give consent for emergency medical treatment necessary during the event?
Yes/No

For further information please do not hesitate to contact youth office on

....

GETTING TO KNOW EACH OTHER ...

1 NAMES

A quick and simple icebreaker that encourages young people to look at the possible links between their names and their cultural or family history.

AIM

To find out the names of a new group that you plan to work with, asking the young people to provide you with a reason to remember them!

YOU WILL NEED

- Nothing

HOW TO DO IT

Ask the young people to form a circle. Place yourself and your co-worker within the group at a distance away from each other.

Explain that you would like each member of the group to introduce themselves and then tell you a bit about the history of their name. This could be the reason they were called it, whether they like it or if they use a nickname instead. Tell them that you are really bad at remembering names and this will help jog your memory for next time!

If everybody looks a bit blank at this stage introduce yourself and demonstrate what you are asking the group to do. For example, you could say something really simple like 'My name is Elizabeth and I was named after my grandmother', or you may wish to share something more elaborate such as 'My name is Elizabeth because my mother really idolises the Queen – my brothers are called Charles and Andrew!'. Finally, you could use the opportunity to introduce a nickname 'My name is Elizabeth, but I hate it – only my mother calls it me! Everyone else calls me Beth'.

Most young people can think of something to share with the group and this is a safe way to tell a little about you without giving too much away!

2 INTRODUCTION CIRCLE

This form of introduction works well with all ages, but for the best effect you need plenty of space to sit down and spread out a bit.

AIM

To introduce the group to each other and the youth workers.

YOU WILL NEED

- A ball of brightly coloured string or wool

HOW TO DO IT

Make a large circle, placing the youth workers apart within the group.

Keeping a hold of one end, the person holding the string throws it to another member of the group to welcome them and introduce themselves. For example, 'Welcome to the group, my name is Krishna'. The second person then replies 'Welcome Krishna, my name is Hattie' and throws it to the next member. This continues until each person has been welcomed and introduced. You may want to make some groundrules about this with the group before you start so that no-one gets left out.

As the exercise progresses you will begin to see a web forming. This is a visualisation of the process. Be really sensitive here to anyone who looks like they are feeling excluded. Ask the young people to look at and reflect on the web they have made.

Finally, ask the young people to put the string down in front of them onto the ground and step away. From this you can all see the interaction of the group.

3 MY DESERT ISLAND

You can use this method of 'mapping' with young people of any age or gender and it works just as well in a group or individually. As it uses pictures it is ideal to use to engage with young people who find writing difficult.

AIM

To begin to understand the important people in the life of the young person.

YOU WILL NEED

- Flipchart paper
- Marker pens
- Stickers, glitter, string, etc. (optional)

HOW TO DO IT

Explain to the group that you are giving them a once in a lifetime opportunity to create their own personal desert island! Go on to say that they can take anyone they like to the island, including friends, family and even pets!

Hand out the paper and art equipment. Make sure you point out that this is not a drawing class, it does not matter if they use pictures, words or a mixture of both.

Allow about 15 minutes for the group to make their selections, draw their island and start to place people where they want them. Be sensitive to who is represented on the island and how young people approach the task.

Next ask them to show where they would like to be.

Finally, tell them they can put anyone they don't want on their island into the sea! You can enlarge upon this by introducing sharks into the water, or boats to bring those they like to see occasionally to visit the island.

Once everyone has finished ask the group if they would like to share their island with the other young people. If there is reluctance to share in the large group you could do this part in pairs. Are there similar choices for who is chosen? Who stays on the island and who is in the sea? Who do they want to be with?

4 HANGMAN

This uses a game that most young people have played at some time as an icebreaker. You can use it with any size group, although with large groups you are unlikely to have the time for all the young people to have a turn.

AIM

To encourage young people to introduce something about themselves that they think identifies them.

YOU WILL NEED

- Flipchart paper and pens

HOW TO DO IT

Decide what theme you are going to set for the game of hangman. This could be a word or short sentence to outline a physical description, a like or dislike, ambition or personal achievement. It could be a 'like' such as dancing or an achievement such as hockey captain or a physical attribute such as dreadlocks or pierced nose that the young person thinks others associate with them. Make sure that the entire group is clear about what you are asking for before you start.

Ask for a volunteer to go first. If there are any young people who do not know how to play, ask one of the others to explain.

The volunteer then puts the appropriate dots and dashes in place of letters to represent words on a large sheet of flipchart paper.

The rest of the group in turn calls out letters, for example 'a', if it is in the word the volunteer writes it in. If not the volunteer should write it down at the side of the sheet. Up to ten wrong guesses are allowed before the group has run out of time and the volunteer shares their puzzle. A guess can be made at any time, but if it is incorrect the person who guessed is out and cannot make any further attempts for that turn.

The person who solves the puzzle correctly goes next and sets their own task for the group to solve.

After a few goes any pattern or similarities that are being established can be discussed with the group.

5 PERSONALITY PLATES

This is a fun way of encouraging a new group to share things about themselves and to get an idea of people's likes and dislikes.

AIM

To produce a collage plate that depicts each group member's personality.

YOU WILL NEED

- Large paper plates
- Glue
- Scissors
- Marker pens
- Newspaper
- Magazines
- Varnish

HOW TO DO IT

Make sure you have a good range of magazines and pictures before the young people arrive – there is nothing worse than discovering the only pictures you have to offer them for their collage are better suited to people over 65!

Suggest that the young people work in groups of four and hand out scissors, glue, magazines and paper plates.

Explain to the group that the idea is for each person to produce a plate that represents their personality. This can include the good and bad bits! Offer a few examples, e.g. a picture of their favourite team if they like football, or pictures that show how they may be feeling today. If the young people look a bit unsure you and your co-worker could have a go at making one too.

Once everyone has finished invite the young people to display their plates, sharing the bits they feel comfortable with to introduce themselves to the group.

Finally, when the glue has dried, varnish the plates to seal the pictures and use them to decorate the group area.

6 'A' NAME GAME

This is a good icebreaker for large groups of young people of any age. You can set themes or restrictions to make the game as easy or as hard as you like!

AIM

To start a session by introducing the group to each other and the youth workers.

YOU WILL NEED

- Nothing!

HOW TO DO IT

Ask the young people to form a circle facing each other.

Explain that what you want is for each person to say their name and use an adjective to describe themselves. There is a catch! It has to be positive and it has to be a word that begins with the same letter as their name. Finally, no-one can duplicate the adjectives no matter how many people there are in the group with the same name!

If you think the group will be shy about this, start the process off yourself and encourage the young people to be as creative as they can. This is usually a fairly easy activity ... unless your name is Zoey and she assures me that the only adjective you can use is 'zany'!

You can vary this by asking the group to introduce their name and an animal they like that starts with the same letter. For example, 'My name is Cerys and I like cats' or 'My name is Zoey and I like zebras'.

Go around the circle until everybody has introduced himself or herself.

7 CLAPPING GAME

This introduction to a session works best with large groups of young people who do not know each other well. Once again, you can make it harder by speeding up the pace as you go around the group.

AIM

The aim of the game is to go around the circle introducing the group to each other and the youth workers.

YOU WILL NEED

- Nothing!

HOW TO DO IT

Ask the young people to make a large circle, standing about arms length apart and then sit down.

Start off the game yourself by clapping twice and saying your name. Each young person then does the same. Place your co-worker somewhere in the second half of the circle so that they can help maintain the rhythm.

Once the circle is completed, start again. This time slapping twice on your knees, clap hands twice and motion to yourself, say your name and then motion to the person on your left and introduce them.

Continue around the group so that everyone introduces themselves and someone else.

If anyone makes a mistake they are out and need to put their legs out in front of them into the circle. The group carries on until only the person who remembers the most names is left.

You can repeat this again at the next group meeting to see how many names have been remembered!

8 GET KNOTTED!

This is a really fun group icebreaker for groups of eight and more. It is a good way to start a session around trust and friendship as team effort is required to be successful!

AIM

This activity encourages young people to start to work together to achieve a group goal.

YOU WILL NEED

- Nothing!

HOW TO DO IT

Ask the group to make a circle, standing next to each other but not so close that they are touching.

Then tell the young people to join hands with two other members of the circle, but not with anyone standing next to them. This is a lot harder than it seems!

Allow about ten minutes for everyone to be included, making sure that no-one is cheating and everyone is holding onto two other people.

When everybody is in place ask the group to stop, hold the pose and look about them to see what shape the group has formed.

Then set the young people the task of untying themselves and reforming the circle - without breaking hands!

You should end up with the whole group back in a circle, though not necessarily all facing the same way!

9 SWAMP GAME

Although this is a team building activity I think it is most effective with young people who have met a few times and begun to work together as a group.

AIM

To complete a task by working together to achieve a common goal.

YOU WILL NEED

- Sheets of newspaper (broadsheets are best)

HOW TO DO IT

Divide the group into teams of three or four.

Set the scene by telling the young people that the distance between the furthest walls of the room is a swamp filled with mud and quicksand. You can be as creative as you like about this bit!

Now, explain that the only way across the swamp is by using the magic sheets that you are about to hand out – but the magic only works if all the team gets over. If the group leaves anyone behind the magic goes and they all fall in the mud!

Hand out sheets of newspaper. You usually only need about six sheets, but if you have a really large hall you will have to allow more. Check first!

Start the teams off – first group to get all their members across the swamp wins!

10 FEELINGS

I have used this with small groups of young people who already know each other and feel comfortable discussing emotions together.

AIM

To explore feelings and how they affect the way people behave.

YOU WILL NEED

- Copies of the 'Feelings' sheet
- Pens

HOW TO DO IT

Ask the young people to choose a partner each. If there is an uneven number in the group work in threes.

Hand out pens and a copy of the 'Feelings' sheet to each member of the group.

Explain that during this exercise individuals are free to choose how much they want to share and have the right to withhold things they do not want to discuss. This gives everyone the opportunity to be as selective as they want.

Ask the young people to look at the sheet on their own to begin with and to put a tick next to ten words that express how they feel when they feel good and a cross next to ten words that describe feeling bad.

When everyone has had time to think about the task and select words that reflect how they feel ask him or her to share their sheet with their partner.

Spend time comparing and discussing what has been written. Are they similar? Expand upon what situations these feelings might be associated with. Ask the young people to discuss how they handle different situations, for example, shyness or excitement.

Close the session by asking the group to each choose one word from the sheet that describes how they feel now.

FEELINGS

These words best describe my feelings

Angry
Embarrassed
Responsible
Unsupported
Shy
Confident
Free
Worried
Secure
Happy
Talkative
Loved
Bored
Unfit
Humiliated
Frightened
Innocent
Stressed
Trusting
Attractive
Affectionate
Unambitious
Guilty
Unwanted
Independent
Bullied
Friendly
Blamed
Superior
Jealous
Wanted
Strong
Lonely
Depressed
Appreciated
Energetic
Unloved
Hurt
Bold
Uneasy
Aggressive
Competitive
Contented
Relaxed

11 THE PRESSURES TODAY!

This activity works with groups of up to six young people of any age. You do need to be sensitive to gender and personal space boundaries when you agree who volunteers to be drawn around and who is doing the drawing.

AIM

To produce a discussion point around the pressures on young people and the sources of stress.

YOU WILL NEED

- A very large sheet of paper
- Assortment of marker pens

HOW TO DO IT

Lay the sheet out on the floor in the middle of the group. Ask one of the young people to volunteer to lie flat on the paper and be drawn around by another member of the group. This part will need to be facilitated carefully.

Once they have finished ask the young person to stand up. You should now have a life-size silhouette to work with.

Ask the young people to take a pen and in turn think of a concern or pressure that young people experience and draw an arrow to show it on the silhouette.

Encourage the group to think about all aspects of a young person's life and discuss each point as it is raised. Is it a universal problem? Is it a problem that is specifically age related? Are there choices or solutions that other members of the group can suggest? Who would they talk to if this was their problem? Discuss support networks and the role of friends.

12 I WENT TO THE NORTH POLE ...

This is one of those silly games that always seems to go down well! I have used it with a wide age range - older young people join in even if they seem reluctant at first! The larger the group the harder the task ...

AIM

The game uses body language and encourages the young people to be observant and to look as well as listen to what is being said.

YOU WILL NEED

- Nothing

HOW TO DO IT

Before the young people arrive set up a large circle of chairs.

Once everyone is seated and can easily see each other either you or another youth worker begins the game by saying 'I went to the North Pole and I bought ... a Christmas tree' or 'a football' or 'a tiger' or 'a bunch of flowers'. It can be absolutely anything, but while saying it you either cross your legs or fold your arms.

The game is about not only listening to what is said but also watching who says it. As you go around the circle the rest of the group have to respond 'yes you did' or 'no you didn't' depending if the right body language is copied. Make sure you seat your co-worker somewhere in the middle of the group so that if no-one has got the idea yet they can demonstrate again.

Once the young people begin to catch on to what they should be doing to get a 'yes' answer they must not tell those who have not yet worked out the pattern.

Keep going around the circle building up a huge and usually increasingly ridiculous list of things collected from the North Pole until everyone has sussed it out!

13 AT WHAT AGE CAN YOU ...?

This quiz is a good introduction to work around young people's rights. It should promote discussion and highlight areas of concern for the group that you may like to explore further.

AIM

To test out young people's knowledge around the law and how it affects them.

YOU WILL NEED

- Pens
- Copies of the quiz sheet (photocopied without the answers!)

HOW TO DO IT

Hand out pens and a copy of the 'At what age can you ...?' sheet.

Ask the young people to work individually on the quiz and to make a guess at anything they do not know the exact answer to.

Allow around 20 minutes, depending on the size of the group.

Form a circle or gather the group together so you can talk without shouting the answers.

Reading aloud ask the group to suggest what age they think it is legal for young people to engage in the activities mentioned.

Take time to discuss any points raised or to answer any questions.

Once the quiz is complete ask the group to count up their scores. How aware of their rights are the young people? Are there any surprises? Which question did most get wrong?

Review to see if additional information or further issue-based sessions are needed.

AT WHAT AGE CAN YOU ...?

1 Have your fingerprints taken by the police .... 10+

2 Give consent or refuse medical or dental treatment 16

3 Be tattooed 18

4 Adopt a child 21

5 Leave home (without your parents' consent) 18

6 Buy fireworks 18

7 Ride a moped (up to 50cc) 16

8 Buy a pet 12

9 Change your name 16
(with parents' consent, 18 without)

10 Consent to sex .... no age of consent for lesbian couples, 18 for gay and 16 for heterosexual

11 Have alcohol taken off you by the police in a public place U18

12 Drink beer or cider with a meal .... 16+

13 Gamble on slot machines .... Any age

14 Buy Lottery tickets or scratch cards 16

15 Be prosecuted for not wearing a passenger seatbelt in a car .... 14+

16 Sit on a jury 18

17 Become a Member of Parliament 21

Source: *Young Citizens Passport 1999/00*

14 REFLECTIVE LISTENING

This introduces the concept of reflective listening to the group. You can use the activity with any size group as the young people are asked to work in threes or fours.

AIM

To focus the group on a discussion which will enable them to get to know each other quickly. If the young people are already friends then it should highlight things that they don't know about each other. It encourages the young people to listen carefully to what is being said and reflect on it, rather than cutting in with their own opinions.

YOU WILL NEED

- Nothing

HOW TO DO IT

Depending on the numbers of young people you have in the group ask them to work in threes or fours. If it is a really small group it does work in pairs. Discuss confidentiality at this stage and reach an agreement that what is shared in the group stays there. This should encourage the participants to feel safe about talking personally.

Specify a topic to discuss within the group: 'What people usually think about me when they first meet me is ...' You can demonstrate this by giving an example to start them off: 'What people think about me when they first meet me is that I have a good sense of humour!' If you think that the group might be nervous choose something less personal like 'one thing I really hate/like is ...'

Set a groundrule that only one member can talk at a time in the group and that the others should listen and think about what is being said.

Once each person has had their say, have a discussion within the groups. How similar was what your friend said to what you actually thought when you first met them? Does your self-image correspond to what others think of you?

Feedback anything that the small groups wish to share with the larger group. Are there similar themes and issues?

15 COLOURS

This activity encourages young people to discuss their feelings and emotions. It can be used with groups of any age, and is most effective with no more than eight people in the group.

AIM

To look at colours and the feelings associated with them.

YOU WILL NEED

- Pens
- Squares of card in assorted colours

HOW TO DO IT

Begin the session by introducing the idea that colours can represent feelings and emotions. Make sure that you stress that this is not an exact science! Different colours may mean different things to different people. A good example of this is the colour red can mean anger or passion.

Once the group has grasped the idea ask them to form smaller groups or work in pairs.

Hand out a good selection of coloured squares with a pen to each pair. Ask the young people to look carefully at the squares and think about what feelings or emotions they associate with the colours. Then write the word on the colour.

If a colour evokes a different response from each partner, write both words on the card.

When everybody has finished ask the whole group to form a circle and discuss their findings. Is there any pattern or theme emerging? Are there many cards with two or more words on? What colours would the group choose to decorate a room to relax in? To dance in? To work in?

Finally ask each young person to choose a colour to represent how they feel now to close the session.

16 NEWSPAPER GAME

This is a simple team game that invites young people to work together to achieve a common task. It is a versatile icebreaker as you can change the subject to suit the project you are working on.

AIM

To work in small groups to complete the challenge set as quickly as possible.

YOU WILL NEED

- A copy of a newspaper for each group
- Scissors
- Glue
- Flipchart paper
- Pens

HOW TO DO IT

You will need to prepare for the game by finding a newspaper that contains articles about young people. This is not usually very difficult! Remember you need a copy for each group so it needs to be current.

Write the task onto a sheet of flipchart but keep this hidden until you have outlined the game to the young people.

When the young people arrive divide them into groups of four and hand out a copy of the newspaper, scissors, glue and a sheet of flipchart paper to each group.

Then explain that the aim of the game is to complete the task you are about to set as quickly as possible by working as a team.

The task is to find:

1. **An article that depicts young people in a positive way.**
2. **An article that depicts young people in a negative way.**
3. **An advert aimed at the youth market.**
4. **Positive images of young people with disabilities.**
5. **Stereotypical articles / pictures of young men.**
6. **Positive role models for young women.**

You can change these to suit the session you have prepared or to follow a theme such as drugs or young people and sport.

Stick the sheet up on the wall so that the young people can refer to it as they look through the papers.

Once they have found the articles each group then makes them into a collage on the flipchart sheet. Pens can be used to add words or put headings.

The group that completes the task first sticks their sheet up and the game ends. A volunteer then shares with the other groups what they found and explains the collage.

Review the process with the group. What was easier to find, negative or positive images?

17 FAMOUS PAIRS

To make this work properly you need to be able to rely on the group to follow the rules and not cheat! The more young people you have the longer and more difficult the game is. It works well with any age or gender.

AIM

To encourage a new group to begin to talk to each other and start to interact.

YOU WILL NEED

- Post-it notes with the names of famous pairs on

HOW TO DO IT

Use Post-it notes to write the names of famous pairs on in advance of the session you have planned. Make sure you take some spare ones in case you get more for your group than you anticipate! Examples of this are Tom & Jerry, Noel & Liam, Beavis & Butthead, etc. Variations on this could be landmarks and places, e.g. Big Ben & London, or sports and sports personalities, e.g. Tanni Grey & athletics.

Once everyone has arrived stick a name on each person's back. Make sure that they can't see what their own new identity is!

Now, ask the group to try and find their pair. To do this they have to go around the room asking questions about the name on their own back. The catch is that they can only ask questions that can be answered 'yes', 'no' or 'don't know'! For example, they can ask 'Am I male?', but not 'Am I a man or woman?'. This is quite hard at first but the group should get the hang of it fairly quickly. Stress that no-one should cheat by telling each other their identity.

Once participants have discovered whose name they have on their back the next task is to find and join up with their pair.

As the young people find their partner ask them to go sit down and review the process together.

At the end of the game everyone will have had the opportunity to talk with all the members of the group.

18 I LIKE PEOPLE WHO ...

This icebreaker works best with groups of eight and more, with both young people and youth workers taking part.

AIM
To open up dialogue between young people and youth workers. It is fast and fun and is a good way to get to know groups that you have not worked with before.

YOU WILL NEED
- Chairs

HOW TO DO IT
Set up a large circle of chairs spaced fairly well apart, with one less chair than the total number of people participating.

Ask the young people to each find a chair and sit down. A youth worker then stands in the middle of the circle – they are the only person without a chair to begin the game.

The person in the middle then calls out 'I like people who ...' This has to be something true for them as well as potentially true for other members of the group. The idea is to discover likes in common not to be as individual as possible. All those that agree with the statement have to leave their chair, run around the outside of the circle as fast as they can and find another to sit on. The person who does not get a chair in time then goes into the middle and the process starts again.

IDEAS
I like people who ...
- **like Boyzone**
- **support Arsenal**
- **watch MTV**
- **eat chocolate**
- **don't eat meat**

Make sure that everyone in the group is included and that participants don't manipulate the game to isolate others.

The game ends when the young people are exhausted!

19 WINK MURDER

Although you could use this with younger children, it really works best with groups of eight or more young people aged 12+. If you have a really large group you could have more than one wink murderer at a time in the group to make it harder and add to the suspense!

AIM

The aim of this icebreaker is to solve the mystery, and offers young people the opportunity to both participate and facilitate.

YOU WILL NEED

- Chairs, although you could do without if you are working outside

HOW TO DO IT

The group sits on chairs arranged in a circle where they can see each other but are not too close. The facilitator asks them to shut their eyes. While the group can't see, the facilitator walks around the outside of the circle and taps a group member on the shoulder. They then become the wink murderer for this game.

The wink murderer has to discreetly wink at other group members, who when winked at must act out various horrible deaths. They are then out for the rest of the round. Encourage the young people to really show off their ability to over-act here!

If at any time the members of the group that are still alive think they know who the killer is they must raise their hand so the facilitator can stop play. They can then say who they think the murderer is and why. If they are wrong they have to die in a dramatic way too.

The person who guesses correctly then starts the process off again, selects the wink murderer and facilitates the next game.

You can play as many rounds of this as the young people want.

20 ATTITUDE SCALE

This icebreaker is a good way to start work around assertiveness and self-image. Alternatively you can adapt it for use with other projects by changing the subject of your scale.

AIM

To encourage the young people to think about how they see themselves and consider how this compares with how others perceive them.

YOU WILL NEED

- Nothing

HOW TO DO IT

Explain to the young people that the aim of this activity is to develop an attitude scale, to show the personalities within the group ranging from assertive to passive. The scale should form a straight line and include everyone.

Decide which end of your scale is assertive and which end is passive and make sure that the young people are clear about this.

Allow five to ten minutes (depending on the size of the group) for the young people to decide where they think they should stand on the scale. Position yourself on the scale too.

When everybody is comfortable with his or her position on the scale, stop.

Ask the young people to look around them and reflect on what they see. Are there any surprises? Does how they see themselves fit in with other people's perception of them? What about the youth workers? Discuss the positive and negative points of both ends of the scale.

FRIENDSHIP AND PEER GROUPS ...

21 IN THE NEWS TODAY

AIM

The aim of this session is to promote a group discussion about a newspaper article that portrays the behaviour of young people.

YOU WILL NEED

- To collect a selection of media stories from magazines, local and national newspapers that feature groups of young people – for example, local gangs, drugs, etc
- Flipchart
- Markers

HOW TO DO IT

Start the session with a group brainstorm onto flipchart paper about how the young people think 'youths' are shown on TV and in the media. List all points, both positive and negative.

Then break the large group into fours and hand a copy of a news story to each smaller group. Give the young people flipchart paper and markers to write points raised on.

Allow 20 minutes for the young people to discuss the story asking them to consider the following:

- **How has the media presented this story?**
- **What message does it give?**
- **How does this reflect on young people?**

Encourage the group to list the main points raised to share back in the large group.

Once everyone is back together ask for a volunteer from each four to outline the issues on their flipchart. Are these similar regardless of the story studied? Facilitate a discussion around the findings. Are different subjects reported in different ways? Are they representative of all young people? How could this change? What can they do as individuals?

You can then plan follow-up sessions dependent on the issues raised.

22 FRIENDSHIP LINE

This is a good way to look at friendships past and present and the importance of them to our own history. It works well with small groups of young men or women.

AIM
To encourage each young person to create a friendship line which charts important people and their influences on their life.

YOU WILL NEED
- Sheets of flipchart paper
- Marker pens

HOW TO DO IT
Hand each member of the group a sheet of flipchart paper and place a good selection of markers close by.

Explain to the young people that they are going to make a friendship line to depict people whose friendship has been important to them from their earliest memories to the present. This can be done using words or pictures.

Next to each name ask the group to show why that person was/is important to them.

While explaining the task, stress that it is up to each person to choose how much they wish to put onto paper and share. Also point out that it does not matter how many or few people are recorded on the line - this is an exercise to look at friendships and what they mean, not a competition to see who knows the most people!

Once everyone has finished ask the group to come together and talk through the parts of their friendship line they feel comfortable sharing. Are there similarities? Have people kept in touch with their early friends? Are some friendships associated with different activities, for example, sports?

23 CHAIN ARGUMENT

This activity comes with a warning! Although it offers young people a forum to experience controlled arguments and compliments in equal measure you need to be very careful at setting and maintaining boundaries so that it does not become an opportunity for destructive comments and bullying.

AIM

To encourage the young people to reflect on the process that leads to conflict and also that which produces compliments. The idea is for the young people to decide whether it is easier to criticise others or to see their good points. There is no wrong or right answer as it is personal and up for discussion!

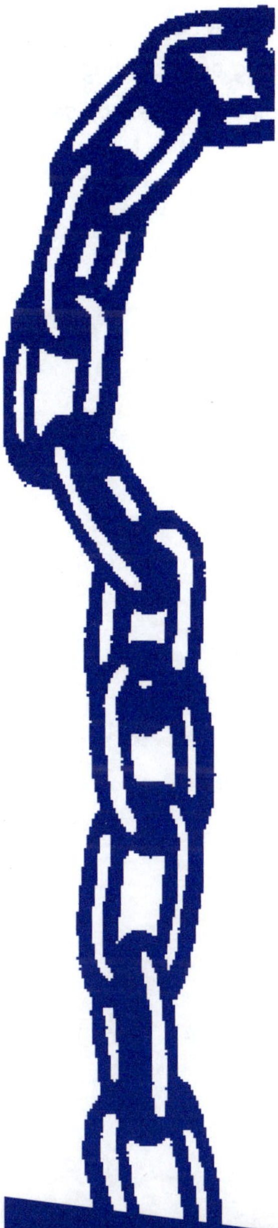

YOU WILL NEED

- Nothing

HOW TO DO IT

Designate an area as a 'stage'. Explain to the group that the object of the activity is to experience conflict and compliments and then discuss what feels the most comfortable – to give or receive? Try to give an idea of the exercise without giving too much away to avoid the group becoming reserved about what they do.

Set some groundrules with the group:

1 Any conversation that takes place ends when the young person comes off stage.

2 Any 'argument' started must be abstract and not a continuation of any outside grievance or vendetta!

3 Only two people can be on stage at any time and the dialogue only takes place for as long as they want – at any time they can withdraw and the next person has a go.

4 If the experience becomes uncomfortable at any time the group stops and reviews what is going on.

They can then add to these if they wish.

Invite two members of the group to begin. Explain that one young person should stand on the stage while the next one approaches them and begins an 'argument'. If there is reluctance or uncertainty about doing this demonstrate what you mean by starting off the process with your co-worker. Be sure to make it clear that this should not be too personal. A good example is to begin with something that may be emotive but not too sensitive: 'So why do you support Tottenham Hotspur then? They're rubbish.' You should then carry on until one person has had enough and leaves the stage.

The next young person joins the remaining group member on the stage and begins a new argument. If at any time this looks to be getting too personal – stop!

When everybody has had the opportunity to participate ask the group to begin the process again, only this time instead of picking an argument with someone they need to compliment or say something positive about them. Once again this will need to be managed carefully.

At the end of the process discuss with the young people how they felt. What was easier? Arguing or complimenting? What felt the most comfortable – the giving or receiving of either? Remember to stress that there is no right or wrong here. You may be surprised at the answers!

24 MIRROR IMAGE

This activity works on the assumption that how we see ourselves and how we are seen by others can be very different. You will need to be sensitive to the group dynamics and make sure no-one uses this as an opportunity to make individuals feel uncomfortable or excluded.

AIM

The idea of the activity is to start young people exploring the idea that how they perceive themselves is not necessarily how others view them. It encourages discussion around public image and first impressions and questions the importance of this.

YOU WILL NEED

- 2 x copies of the 'Mirror image' sheet for each participant (in two different colours)
- Pens

HOW TO DO IT

Explain the aim of the session to the group and ask the young people to choose a partner to work with. Hand each person two copies of the 'Mirror image' sheet (one of each colour) and a pen.

Now ask them to turn away from their partner and have a brief look at the sheet. Working with their back to their partner ask each person to compete both sheets:

Sheet 1:
Tick all the boxes alongside words that they think describe the young person they are working with.

Sheet 2:
Tick all the boxes next to words that they think describe themselves.

Allow up to 15 minutes for everybody to complete the task, and then ask the young people to turn around and face their partner. Each partner in turn then feeds back what they have ticked and compares this with how their partner sees him or herself. Are these the same? Are characteristics seen in different ways? For example, a young person may have ticked 'assertive' about himself or herself, but their partner sees this as 'aggressive'. Encourage the young people to focus on positive attributes and discuss areas of difference.

Bring the whole group back together and facilitate a discussion around first impressions, drawing on the issues raised through the sheets but not focusing on individuals.

MIRROR IMAGE

Think about the words below - which ones apply to you? Put a tick in the appropriate box.

Honest		Assertive		Sporty	
Creative		Sarcastic		Funny	
Independent		Happy		Outrageous	
Dependable		Aggressive		Embarrassing	
Loner		Trusting		Tolerant	
Controlling		Shy		Sensitive	
Spiteful		Tough		Unhappy	
Gentle		Outgoing		Loud	
Easily-led		Greedy		Untruthful	
Quiet		Moody		Clever	
Cheeky		Lazy		Leader	
Stubborn		Worrier		Romantic	
Practical		Open		Sympathetic	
Jealous		Kind		Generous	
Mean		Careful		Secretive	
Bossy		Loyal		Trustworthy	
Ambitious		Nosy		Mature	
Popular		Adventurous		Careless	

25 I HEARD ...

This is a new take on the old game Chinese Whispers. It effectively shows what happens as a sentence or gossip is passed within a group. You will need more than ten young people for it to work really well.

AIM

The idea is to demonstrate how what is said can be distorted as it is being told from person to person.

YOU WILL NEED

- Nothing – apart from a complicated sentence that you can think up in advance!

HOW TO DO IT

Ask the group to form a big circle. Make sure there is a distance between each member so that they will have to lean across to each other to pass on the gossip you are going to start.

When they are ready move towards the young person next to you in the circle and whisper the sentence that you prepared earlier. Try and make this as real life as possible: 'Did you know that ...?!' Make sure that it is fairly long and complicated so that the opportunities for it to be misheard are good!

Wait until it has been whispered through the whole group and then ask the last person to repeat what they heard. It should be somewhat different to what you said at the start.

Discuss the differences and then ask the young people to reflect on examples in real life where something that they have said has been misconstrued or not understood. How did that feel? Could they give out the right information easily? Have they ever passed on gossip that turned out to be untrue? What happened?

26 IF I COULD CHOOSE ...

This should be done quickly to get open responses and works with any size group. You can change your topic to suit the age and interests of the group.

AIM

To begin to focus the group on things that are important to them in a friend and promote discussion on positive relationships.

YOU WILL NEED

- Nothing

HOW TO DO IT

Gather the group together and ask them to form a circle. This means that you can all see each other and should be able to hear what is said.

Explain to the group that the idea of this activity is to start to think about what makes a good friend. Ask the young people to think about which soap opera character they would choose to be their friend if they could. Encourage the group to think about why they would make a good friend.

Once everyone has decided ask him or her to turn to the person on their right and share their choice. For example, 'If I could choose a character in a soap to be a friend I would choose Sonia from *EastEnders* because she always listens to people'.

You can change the topic to anything that you think that the group will engage with, for example:

- Character in a book 'I would choose ... because ...'
- Person in a movie 'I would choose ... because ...'
- Cartoon character 'I would choose ... because ...'

Invite the young people to share what they have talked about in pairs with the main group and facilitate a discussion. Are there similar suggestions? Are some ideas based only on how the character looks, e.g. 'I would choose Jamie from EastEnders because he looks really good and has a car'. Is this a good basis for choosing a friend?

Pull out the main themes and ideas about what makes a character a good friend. Are these realistic things to want in a relationship? Do the young people consider that they offer these things to their friends? What are the differences?

27 MAD, SAD, BAD OR GLAD?

Even if you usually find it hard to engage a group in drama-based games, the name of this activity is so brilliant the young people are bound to be intrigued enough to give it a go!

AIM

To look at how we use body language to communicate how we feel. The exercise is also a good way to raise levels of personal awareness within a group and highlight the impact individuals have on others.

YOU WILL NEED

- Chalk

HOW TO DO IT

With the chalk mark four spaces on the ground – MAD, SAD, BAD and GLAD. Make sure that you leave enough space for the young people to stand by a particular 'feeling' clearly.

Explain to the group that each area marked shows a different feeling. You can go on to talk about how in the same situation feelings may differ within a group, and how we often hide our true feelings.

Ask for a volunteer to select the area that most represents how they feel today. If there is reluctance to go first, ask your co-worker to demonstrate.

The rest of the group then gathers round (not too close!) and asks questions about why they have chosen that space. These should be supportive, not accusations or aggressive. For example: 'Are you feeling sad?', 'Did something happen at school today to make you feel that way?'

The volunteer can tell the group what is wrong – but cannot speak. This means that they have to rely solely on body language to convey their feelings. Make sure that you are sensitive to the group and do not allow anyone to feel that they are being interrogated!

When they have shared all that is comfortable the volunteer leaves the space and another member of the group takes their place. In a small group each member can experience the process. Make sure that you allow time for feedback and review any issues that are raised.

28 HELPING HAND

This session can be done either as a group or one-to-one activity. It is a good start to a project which is looking at keeping safe and protective behaviour.

AIM

To encourage the young people to identify people they could talk to if they were worried or concerned about an issue.

YOU WILL NEED

- Paper
- Pens

HOW TO DO IT

Before you start consider the make up of your group and how much you know about them. If you have not worked with the group before you will need to be very careful to keep the information discussed depersonalised by referring only to the examples below. If you know the group well you can ask them to think of their own situations. Be careful that you do not encourage the young people to make disclosures unless you have the appropriate support in place.

Ask the group to form a circle or to sit so that they can all hear you and contribute.

Choose one of the situations below and read it out to the young people.

'Tom is 15, wears glasses and is the smallest in his year. He hates sports, but is really good at maths and science so tends to stay in at break time in the IT room so he can use the Internet more. The other kids all laugh and call him "boffin" and "goody-goody" and "teacher's pet" and take his glasses out of his bag and throw them to each other when he leaves school to go home.'

'Cherish is 13 and friends with a big group of girls, most of whom have just started smoking. Because they can't afford cigarettes, most of the girls have been nicking them off parents or asking older kids to get them from the off-licence. Cherish does not smoke, but both her mum and stepdad do. Now the others in the group are saying that they won't hang around with her if she does not steal her share of cigarettes.'

Then ask the question: 'How do you think Tom/Cherish feels?' and facilitate a discussion around the answers given.

Now ask the group to start to imagine that they are in a similar situation. Explain that they do not have to share what they are thinking, but suggest that they start to identify people that they could tell and ask for help.

Hand out the paper and pens and ask each young person to draw around one of their hands in the centre of their sheet.

Now explain that the thumb on the hand represents the first person that they would go to if they were in trouble and needed help. Ask them to write down who they would go to next if the first person wasn't in or would not listen. Carry on until all five fingers have names.

Reflect on the process with the group. Was it easy to identify a support network? Will it change often? What is it about these people that makes them special and different to others they know?

29 STORYTIME

This story is told like a fairy tale, but depicts a scenario that poses questions that are open to interpretation and value judgments. It works with any age and provokes the most discussion in mixed gender groups!

AIM

To open up a discussion around a series of events that highlight love, friendship and betrayal. The story itself is imaginary, but the young people are encouraged to reflect the issues into their own lives and reach conclusions.

YOU WILL NEED

- A copy of the story to read from

HOW TO DO IT

Ask the young people to form a circle or gather together in one group so that they can all hear you.

Introduce storytime - we usually use the old saying 'are you sitting comfortably? Well, then I'll begin' routine, but it will depend on your group how you do this.

Encourage the young people to listen carefully for the twists in the story and each character's part in the events.

Once you have finished reading pose the question: 'So, whose fault is it that the baroness is dead?'

Question observations made and accusations of blame. For example, 'it was her own fault for disobeying her husband!' can be challenged to raise issues around the right of a man to threaten his wife with punishment for disobedience. Explore attitudes - what about the lover? The friend? Who should have offered help in their opinion? Facilitate a discussion that encompasses some of the points raised. This should also enable youth workers to identify any further issue-based work.

STORYTIME

Once upon a time, in a place a long way from here a jealous baron kissed his wife goodbye as he left her to visit his other castles. 'Do not leave the castle while I am gone,' he said. 'If you do I will punish you severely when I return!'

As the hours passed, the young baroness grew sad and lonely. Finally, she felt so alone that she decided to disobey her husband's orders and leave the castle to visit her lover who lived in the forest nearby.

Now, the castle was situated on an island in a wide, fast flowing river and there was only one way to reach the mainland. This was to cross the drawbridge that linked the island to the forest at the narrowest part of the river.

The baroness stood at the edge of the river, 'surely my husband will not return before dawn?' she thought. 'I will have time to visit my lover and get back before him.' With that she ordered her servants to lower the drawbridge and leave it down until she returned.

Having spent several happy hours with her lover the baroness returned to the castle only to find that the drawbridge was blocked by a gateman. The gateman was fiercely waving a long cruel knife and shouted: 'Do not attempt to cross this bridge baroness, or I will have to kill you – it is the baron's orders!'

Fearing for her life the baroness ran back to her lover and asked him to help her. 'But our relationship is only a romantic one,' he explained. 'I thought you knew that? I will not help!'

The baroness ran back to the river and having told her story to the boatman pleaded for his help.

'I will do it,' said the boatman 'but only if you can pay my fee of five marks.'

'Five marks?' exclaimed the baroness. 'But all my money is in the castle! I can pay you later.'

'Hard luck! No money, no ride,' said the boatman flatly and turned away.

Her fear growing the baroness ran crying to her friend and after explaining her desperate situation, begged for enough money to pay the boatman.

The friend shook her head: 'If you had not disobeyed your husband this would not have happened, I will give you no money!'

With the sun rising behind the island and her last attempt to get help refused, the baroness returned sadly to the gate, where she was slain by the gateman as she attempted to reach the castle.

30 HOW ASSERTIVE ARE YOU?

The next two activities can be used together to begin to explore bullying and self-esteem with young people. You can use them with either young men or women, although you may want to alter the questions slightly. However, I have found that it works best with small groups who know each other well enough to be honest.

AIM

To look at the differences between being assertive and aggressive and provoke discussion within the group.

YOU WILL NEED

- Enough copies of the worksheet/quiz for all the group
- Pens

HOW TO DO IT

Hand out a pen and a copy of the quiz to each young person. Explain that you want them to work on their own to begin with, but if you know that some group members will struggle with this suggest pairs.

Introduce the quiz by saying that there are a series of situations and possible responses shown on the page. You want the group to look and tick the response that they feel would be closest to their own reaction in a similar circumstance. Most young people are familiar with quizzes such as this in magazines and will need minimum support at this stage.

Once everyone has finished and is happy with their response to each question ask the group to come together.

Read out the questions and the answers and ask the young people to keep a tally of how many 'a', 'b' and 'c's they have ticked as you go through the sheet.

Finally ask the group to count and see which letter they have ticked the most. Then ask them to refer to the sheet to see where those answers fit. Stress that they do not need to share this analysis unless they feel comfortable doing so.

Encourage feedback and ask the young people questions around what they ticked and why to provoke further discussion. Do they agree with the quiz? Is saying, 'please don't do it' really submissive? How could they be generally more assertive and make their feelings known without being aggressive? What are the advantages/disadvantages of each response?

HOW ASSERTIVE ARE YOU?

Look at the situations and responses below. Some are aggressive, some are submissive and some are assertive. Which one sounds most like you?

1 **You are standing in a queue for the bus and someone pushes in front of you, do you:**

a) say nothing, they may have a go at you

b) tap them on the shoulder and politely explain to them where the back of the queue is

c) shove past them when the bus arrives and stare hard at them if they look like saying something

2 **You are at the hairdressers and she doesn't cut your fringe straight, do you:**

a) refuse to pay and have a loud argument with the stylist, after all she is supposed to be a professional

b) manage to get outside before you burst into tears – you're going to have to wear a hat for ages

c) ask the stylist to check if your fringe is straight as it looks wrong to you – if you are right you will ask her to straighten it

3 **Your best mate wants to go to a club that stays opens until 3am – your mum says you have to be in at 12.00, but your friend wants to stay all night, do you:**

a) go, although you know you won't enjoy it because you have promised your mum, but she is your friend ...

b) explain to her that you have given your mum your word, but you will go with her until you need to leave – if she is your friend she will respect your promise too

c) tell her that no-one tells you what to do and get home at 5am, you can handle your mum

4 **You are with a friend who you know has been shoplifting around the town at weekends. Suddenly in the supermarket she suggests you have a go too, you say 'no' but she keeps on pushing you, do you:**

a) shout, 'when I say no, I mean no' and threaten to hit her if she keeps on

b) take her to one side and quietly say 'when I say no, I mean no', then walk away

c) say 'I'm sorry I can't do it, please don't be angry with me' – you don't want to lose your friend

5 **You go to the cinema and your date suggests you go see a film that you know you will hate, do you say:**

a) 'Oh all right, I don't mind going if you want to', even though you hate action movies and really wanted to see something else

b) 'I really don't want to see this film – can't we choose one we both like? You can always see this with your friends another time'
c) 'No way am I going in to see that! If you insist you can go on your own!'

6 You are walking down the corridor at school and two people from your class laugh as you go past, do you:
a) turn around, walk back and confront them – who do they think they are laughing at?
b) turn where you are and say 'please don't laugh at me like that, I don't like it'
c) walk back to where they are standing to check out if they are laughing at you and then tell them to stop, you've had enough

7 You buy a top from a shop, but when you get home you notice it has a button missing, do you:
a) ask your mum to take it back – how embarrassing!
b) take it back with the receipt the next day and ask for an exchange
c) go back in with all your mates and let rip about the rubbish they are trying to sell – that will teach them!

8 At the youth club all your mates are slagging off one of the CDs being played – it's yours! Do you:
a) own up – you don't care, you think it's great
b) laugh along with the rest and hope that the youth worker doesn't hand it back to you while they're looking
c) feel really angry and start an argument – who's criticising you now?

Mainly 'a'
These reactions are submissive; you don't always need to go along with everyone else! There is nothing wrong with being you and making your feelings and opinions known. You need to look at ways to give clearer messages that reflect what you really want.

Mainly 'b'
You are comfortable with being 'assertive', while remaining sensitive to other people's needs. You expect people to respect who you are and offer respect back. Make sure that you maintain this even when things get difficult!

Mainly 'c'
Steady there! You will find that people are more ready to listen to your point of view if you give them space and look at other ways to get your message across rather than getting angry and loud. You may be right but no-one will listen if you don't calm down!

31 WHAT IS BULLYING?

This encourages the young people you are working with to think about the different forms that bullying can take. It can be used with the previous quiz to form part of an ongoing project around self-image and personal esteem.

AIM

To offer a starting point for young people to discuss bullying and the effects that it has on both the victim and the bully.

YOU WILL NEED

- Two sets of the 'What is bullying?' cards
- Contact numbers and leaflets for local support groups

HOW TO DO IT

In two groups ask the young people to read the set of cards you are handing out. Explain that both groups will have the same information on their cards.

Ask the young people to assess each of the situations outlined on the cards and as a group agree whether they depict a bullying situation or not. You will need to be sensitive to any young person within the group that you suspect or know has been a victim of bullying.

When the young people have had a chance to discuss the situations and reach agreement, bring everybody together in a large group.

Read out each of the cards and ask the two groups what they decided. Is it the same? Facilitate a discussion over each card – what could the young person have done if they were being bullied? What would they do if it happened to them? Why do they think people become bullies? Discuss protective tactics and strategies for being assertive in bullying situations. Make sure that the young people have information and contact numbers for support, including someone to tell if they feel that they are a victim.

WHAT IS BULLYING

'I have told her before, the reason I shout is so I don't hit her ... I can't say fairer than that can I?'	'Ben says that if I want him to keep quiet about it I have to give him my dinner money all of next week'
'Miss Betts always picks on me - she knows I don't have the answer but she likes making me cry in front of the class'	'The boss at my Saturday job keeps putting his arms round me when he shows me how to work the till - it is really revolting'
'I like football but we have to get off the pitch when the older boys come out'	'My dad always asks me to do the washing up - never my brother'
'Orla says that if I want a boyfriend I had better lose some weight and get rid of my spots'	'My boyfriend says that if I love him I will stay at his house when his parents are away - I am scared'
'Kelly keeps following me about, I try ignoring her but she won't get the hint'	'Every time I walk past Mark and his mates they all laugh at me and call me shorty'
'If she wants to come out with me she will have to lend me her new top, otherwise she can go on her own'	'That bus driver always shouts at us when we get on his bus - last night he only let half of us on'
'Have you seen Daryl in PE? What a sight, we all laugh as he comes into the gym!'	'Like maths? No way! I don't want everyone thinking that I'm a boffin'
'I have tried ignoring them, but they just throw things at my back as I walk into youth club'	'I like Daniel, but all my friends will laugh if I go out with him'
'So I told him 'Go out with you? No way' - he would probably want his mummy to come too!'	'It is hard, every time I come out of school one of them is there waiting for me'

32 BEST OF FRIENDS

This is best used with a small group of young women, although you could change the gender in the scenario given and improvise! It is really an exercise that explores what happens next?

AIM

To give focus to a discussion around friendships and the dynamics within a small group. It explores the idea that not everyone is what he or she seems!

YOU WILL NEED

- A copy of the 'Best of friends' scenario

HOW TO DO IT

Ask the young women to gather into a circle and make themselves comfortable – explain you want to tell them a story!

Depending on how well you know the group you can either read the scenario yourself or ask for a volunteer. Make sure you read slowly enough for everyone to get the gist of the story.

Once you have finished ask the following questions to provide a framework for a discussion:

1 Who is the 'real' friend here?
2 Who holds the power in the group?
3 What do you think each young woman should do next?
4 How can they resolve the conflict?

Draw the discussion to a close once a strategy for what happens next has been agreed.

BEST OF FRIENDS

Carly attends the youth club every week. Although she has been excluded from school for bullying and is branded a trouble maker by her former teachers, she has been eager to take part in club sessions and is a reliable and popular member of the group. She is bestfriends with another young woman, Hannah. They tend to do everything as a pair, but Carly appears the leader of the two and generally makes decisions for them both.

Gemma is 15 and has just started to be friends with the two girls. She gets on best with Hannah as Gemma and Carly tend to compete for attention from the young men at the club. Hannah does not really help the situation as she often sides with one friend against the other. This has resulted in arguments and on one occasion Gemma and Carly had a fight over something Hannah told Carly that Gemma had said.

This evening, Gemma is crying in the toilets and Hannah goes to get the youth worker as she is worried something is going to happen. Both young women appear upset and angry. Hannah protectively explains that Carly hates Gemma now and has threatened to 'give her a slapping' if Gemma enters the youth club. Gemma agrees that there is a problem but says she does not know why Carly dislikes her so much. She explains Hannah says that Carly has accused her of 'stealing' boyfriends and 'sleeping around'. Hannah begins saying that Gemma should stand up for herself more and follows when Gemma suddenly storms off in search of Carly to sort it out.

The youth workers arrive at the pool table in time to hear Gemma shouting abuse at Carly. Carly is repeating her threat to hit Gemma and is waving the pool cue menacingly. Carly tells Hannah to get out of the way, as she has no argument with her and says she will still be her bestfriend as long as she ignores Gemma. As the youth workers try to calm the situation down and get the girls to talk, Hannah turns away from her two fighting friends and smiles to herself.

33 NO MEANS NO!

This encourages young people to develop strategies to say 'no' effectively in difficult situations. I have used it both with small groups and individually. You can vary the exercise by changing the issue featured in the scenario, the storyboard can be used in any context.

AIM

To develop assertiveness in saying 'no' to peer pressure to do things the young people are uncomfortable with.

YOU WILL NEED

- A storyboard sheet for each group
- Pens

HOW TO DO IT

Read out the following situation to the young people. Hand out a copy of the storyboard to each member of the group and make a good selection of pens available. Using their storyboard, ask the young people to show what the character could say or do to resolve the situation.

> **You are in town with two of your mates. As you walk out of one shop they both start laughing and later show you chocolate and sweets they have stolen. They tell you that it is really easy and very safe as the security cameras don't really work. They decide to make another visit to the shop before you all go home and encourage you to take part this time. You don't want anything to do with it. What should you say and do?**

Ask the group to come together and share storyboards. Use this as a basis for a discussion on peer pressure relating back to the given scenario.

Encourage the young people to think about the consequences of the characters' actions. How they could say what they think assertively? What could they have done differently? How easy is it to say 'no' to friends? What could be done to resolve any potential conflict between the group in the story?

Any issues highlighted can be used to plan further sessions.

NO MEANS NO!

Use the storyboard to show what happens next ...

34 MY IDEAL FRIEND

This encourages young people to think about what qualities they look for in a friend, what makes a person special and how to value friendship.

AIM

To identify the key features that makes a trusting friendship.

YOU WILL NEED

- Copies of the 'Ideal friend' sheet
- Pens

HOW TO DO IT

Hand out the 'Ideal friend' sheets and a pen to each member of the group.

Explain that what you want them to do is think about who their ideal friend would be. This can be a real or imagined person but stress that you are asking them to consider personal qualities that they think are vital for a good friendship, not what someone looks like or who is cool to hang out with.

When the young people have had time to think ask them to list the six attributes that they think are the most important. They can do this in order of importance if they want, depending on the group. Ask only that they do this individually at the moment.

Once they have completed the six, ask them to write in the box below the reason why this is a positive attribute and offer an example.

Make sure you allow everyone enough time to think about the task and then ask the group to break into pairs to share ideas. Encourage them to discuss their responses. Are there similarities? Are these realistic things to want in a friend? Are the characteristics that they value in others ones they think describe themselves?

Finally, ask the young people to feed back common themes to develop a group ideal friend.

MY IDEAL FRIEND

Think carefully and list the six characteristics you would want in your ideal friend

1	
2	
3	
4	
5	
6	

Now, consider why these attributes are important to you and any examples you can think of when you would want a friend to be like this

1	
2	
3	
4	
5	
6	

35 WITHOUT OFFENCE

This offers scenarios for young people to explore the more difficult aspects of friendships.

AIM

To promote assertive behaviour and the right to challenge friends.

YOU WILL NEED

- The scenarios on the sheet cut up ready to be handed out

HOW TO DO IT

Ask the young people to get into groups of three or four and hand a different scenario to each. You can add to these to make them specific to any issues within the group.

The young people then choose someone to read out their card and listen to the hypothetical situation depicted.

The task for the group is to discuss the dilemma and agree how to resolve the situation without offending the friend.

Allow 20 to 30 minutes for the young people to discuss the issues and then ask them to come together again when they have a strategy.

Each group then briefly outlines their scenario and explains how they have decided to sort out the problems. Once each group has spoken allow time for this to be challenged or new suggestions made. You can always prompt this by asking whether they should worry about offending the friend, or questioning whether it is a friendship the two young people have. This can then lead to real life experiences being discussed if appropriate.

WITHOUT OFFENCE

You are speaking on the phone to your friend. You only have a few credits left and no money till the end of the week. Your friend starts to tell you for the third time what happened last night with her new boyfriend. How are you going to get off the phone without offending her?

Your friend has borrowed your new CD. You have asked for it back twice but he keeps saying that he has forgotten to bring it with him. It is now a week later and you really want it returned now. How are you going to get it back?

You are getting something out of your friend's bag when you notice a packet of cigarettes. Your friend has always said that she doesn't smoke and has been rude to others who do – how are you going to raise the subject without offending her?

Your friend is loudly telling everyone in the group that she does not believe in sex before marriage and that people who sleep around get a name for themselves. You don't agree at all, but your friend is looking to you for support. What can you do?

Your friend always turns up at youth club with no money. For the last three weeks you have paid for him to get in and bought him a drink. You can't really afford to do this any more as he never offers to pay you back. Club is on tomorrow, how are you going to say something?

36 HOW DO I LOOK?

This activity explores stereotypes and is good to use as an opening session for projects around issues such as gender and self-image. It works effectively with groups of up to eight young people.

AIM

The aim of the session is to raise the group's awareness of stereotyping in a non-confrontational way, encouraging them to open up further discussions.

YOU WILL NEED

- Copies of the 'How do I look?' sheet (cut up)
- Flipchart paper
- Plenty of coloured markers

HOW TO DO IT

Hand each young person a slip from the 'How do I look?' sheet and a piece of flipchart paper. Explain that each slip has on it a word that can be used to describe a person.

Ask them to look at the word on the slip and using marker pens draw a picture of how they think that person looks. Stress that they should not tell anybody else what is on the slip at this stage. Emphasise that this is not a drawing competition and that they can use any style that they like.

Give the group ten minutes to do this and then ask them to stop and gather together with their pictures.

People then show their picture to the rest of the group who try to guess what the description was.

When all the pictures have been correctly identified go back and review what has been drawn. Are all the models shown as women? Are all the racists drawn as men? How about bullies and teacher's pet? Encourage the group to discuss how they decided what gender to draw and question if certain attributes or qualities are seen as gender specific.

HOW DO I LOOK?

BULLY	TEACHER'S PET
COOL	THIEF
RACIST	WIMP
GREEDY	HAPPY
SPORTY	LONELY
LAZY	REBEL
CARING	SHY
TARTY	LOUD MOUTH
FUNNY	MODEL
MEAN	GOSSIP
DJ	FIGHTER

37 MIRROR, MIRROR

This looks at body language and explores the way signals can be transmitted without words. It works well following the icebreaker Feelings that questions how we are seen and how we see ourselves. This can be used as part of an assertiveness project, including bullying and peer pressure.

AIM

To raise young people's awareness of the power of non-verbal communication.

YOU WILL NEED

- Nothing

HOW TO DO IT

Introduce the idea of body language to the group. Ask the group to consider how they think people see them - as a quiet person? Disco diva? Shy? Sarcastic? Then ask the young people to share this with the people sitting either side of them. Are there any surprises or differences? Conclude by asking the group to think about the signals that they give without talking that add or detract from their image. The idea is to explore non-verbal communication further.

Ask the young people to choose a partner to be their 'mirror'. Facing each other, take it in turns to act out a feeling from the list below. You will need to be sensitive to any very shy young people in your group who might find it very difficult to participate. Encourage them to work within their comfort zones, but to have a go.

- Confident
- Anxious
- Bored
- Excited
- Scared
- Angry
- Happy
- Shy
- Interested
- Depressed

When everyone has had the opportunity to be the image and the original, stop and review the process.

Is it easy to see how someone feels? How can this work in difficult situations, for example, when you are scared but want to appear confident? How important is it to make sure that the messages that people give are the correct ones that show how they feel?

38 TO BE A MAN

This looks at how gender is constructed in the tabloid press. It was given to me as part of a project with young men, but you could reverse the gender and use it with young women too.

AIM

To look at the pressures placed on young men to conform to social norms and how the media influences these.

YOU WILL NEED

- A good selection of articles about men from the tabloid press
- Flipchart paper
- Pens

HOW TO DO IT

In preparation for the session collect a good range of articles about men. Try and include international copy and local interest stories as well as clippings from magazines such as *GQ* and *Loaded!*

When the young men arrive hand them two or three articles each. In a circle ask the group to read their articles and to shout out all of the words that are describing men as they see them.

Your co-worker can facilitate this if it becomes a shouting competition! You need to record everything onto the flipchart paper so nothing is missed.

When they have finished ask them to put the articles down and read back to them all the words that have been collected.

Use this as the basis for a discussion. Start by asking the questions: Is this how men really are? Is this how they see themselves? Their friends? The men they know such as their fathers or brothers? Who is a positive role model in their life and why?

Look at this and compare any conflicting images found, e.g. 'the new man' and the 'laddish' culture.

Review and identify any further work with the group for future sessions.

39 BULLY COURT

Before you consider this project you need to be aware of the dynamics within the group you plan to work with. It may not be appropriate for someone who has either been a recent victim of bullying or who already dominates the group.

AIM

To explore the issues around bullying and to look at the different characters' involvement in a given scenario.

YOU WILL NEED

- A set of the 'Bully court' cards
- Leaflets and telephone numbers for local support networks for the victims of bullying

HOW TO DO IT

This is a role play activity which divides up the characters to work through the issues highlighted during the bully court. There are no given solutions as the young people will take the role play where they want to. The facilitator's job is to set the scene, make sure that no-one is feeling uncomfortable and that any issues raised are resolved.

Ask the group to form a circle and then read the following, changing the gender to suit your group.

> **This bully court has come together to assess this situation and agree whether bullying has taken place or not. The court will then decide what should, if anything, happen to the bully.**
>
> **It is alleged that two young men kicked another young person on the way home from school. One then ripped up schoolwork, spat and made further threats if this behaviour was talked about with teachers or parents. This is not the first time that an incident like this has happened. Money has also been stolen from the young person and food taken with the threat of violence if they argued back.**
>
> **The young men say that it is not their fault and that the other young person started all the trouble. They claim that the other young person does not like them and is trying to get them in trouble. Neither will comment on the stealing, spitting and threats of violence.**

Hand out a card with a character name on to each member of the group. Allow ten minutes for each participant to think about the role that they are to play and how this could fit with the scene outlined by the facilitator.

In the meantime set up the room so that the circle you had becomes a semi-circle with one chair at the front for the judge, one for the accused and one for each witness or speaker. The rest of the group will form the jury and make decisions on what happens next based on discussion and consensus. The idea is that this represents a court.

The facilitator then invites each character in turn to step forward and tell their story to the bully court.

In role, the young people can then discuss what has been said and decide whether this is a case of bullying or wrongful accusations.

Finally, facilitate a discussion about what should happen to bullies and how victims of bullying can keep themselves safe and be more assertive.

BULLY COURT

VICTIM You have not told anyone what has been happening to you over the last months as you are scared of what might happen.	**ACCUSED** You are angry because you don't think it is your fault. Lots of people argue - what is all the fuss about?
ACCUSED You do not think that you should be here at all. Everyone always blames you; it's not fair.	**WITNESS** You have seen some things that have made you worried. You do not think that it is right that someone is being picked on.
TEACHER You teach all those involved and have stepped in before.	**WITNESS** You know what has happened but you are scared about what will happen to you if you say something.
JUDGE Your role is to listen to each person and make sure that you and the jury are clear about what is being said.	**PARENT** Your son has never been in trouble before and you don't believe it.
PARENT It is not just at school that your son is difficult. He is angry and aggressive at home too and you have had enough.	**PARENT** You have been getting more and more concerned recently. Your child does not want to go to school, go out, anything.
JURY	**JURY**
JURY	**JURY**
JURY	**JURY**
JURY	**JURY**
JURY	**JURY**

40 CRESTS

This teambuilding activity works well with any age, and is suitable for groups of six or less. Because it does not involve writing it is a useful way of encouraging the whole group to take part.

AIM

To produce a crest that is representative of the group, showing individual as well as shared interests.

YOU WILL NEED

- Dough or plasticine
- Cutting tools (pastry shapes, blunt knives, etc)
- Rolling pins (or empty plastic drink bottles)
- A stiff piece of card for each group
- Cleaning material (to clear up afterwards!)

HOW TO DO IT

In preparation for the session arrange tables with six chairs around them. On each table place dough, cutting tools, rolling pins and a piece of stiff card.

As the young people come in ask them to take a seat at a table. Set a rule that they cannot move the chairs, so if the table is full they must find another seat. This should prevent you ending up with one table of ten and two young people on their own!

Once everyone has a seat explain that the task is for each group to produce a crest that shows the people on their table. It needs to represent characteristics of each individual as well as things that the group has in common. They may want to use the knives to add their names to the crest. Do not be too prescriptive as you want the group to be as creative as possible.

Allow about 30 minutes for the artwork to be completed. It will take longer if you have a lot of groups. Ask the young people to display their crests on the stiff card when they have finished.

Next allow gallery time so that everyone can view all the crests. This is not a competition but an opportunity to share. In turn each group stands by their crest and answers any questions the rest of the young people may have.

Review the process. Were there any common themes? How easy was it to negotiate things that represented everyone? How were individual attributes chosen?

You can then dry or bake the crests and display them in the club. A variation would be to produce a large crest that represents the whole youth club.

41 GROUP FALL

You need to do a risk assessment before you try this one! Make sure you give clear instructions. If the group is too young or does not really understand what you are asking you could end up with an accident!

AIM

To encourage the young people to appreciate the importance of trust in friendships.

YOU WILL NEED

- Nothing

HOW TO DO IT

Ask the young people to form a circle, including yourself and your co-worker. This will need to be fairly close together with enough space to move quickly to successfully complete the task.

Now ask for a volunteer. Be careful here that the first volunteer is not someone universally unpopular within the group or who is very nervous and unlikely to feel comfortable.

Once you have a volunteer invite them to move to the middle of the circle and ask them to close their eyes.

Explain that the idea of the group fall is to highlight the need for trust within relationships and particularly friends. What you are going to do is to ask the young person in the middle to fall, still with their eyes closed, and as a group you are all going to catch them.

Suggest that if the young people decide to let the volunteer fall, they should consider how they would feel if the same thing happened during their turn.

Review the activity as you go along. How does it feel to have your eyes closed and place your trust in your friends? How does it feel to be responsible for the safety of someone else? What feels more comfortable?

Continue the activity until everybody has experienced both roles.

LIVING AT HOME ...

42 FAMILY VALUES

This is an opening session that questions what young people mean by the concept of family.

AIM

The aim of this activity is to highlight that all families are different shapes and sizes but should be valued equally.

YOU WILL NEED

- Nothing

HOW TO DO IT

Explain to the group that you are going to call out a list of statements that you want them to think about and then vote on with their opinion.

The voting system works like this:

- if they agree with the statement they raise both hands in the air;
- if they disagree they keep both hands by their side; or
- if they are not sure or agree in part they raise one hand.

Make sure all the young people can hear you and everyone is clear about how to vote!

After each vote ask the group to look around and challenge each other or ask questions. Make sure that this is done positively and is not an excuse for attacking each other's opinions and values.

Follow up any issues identified in further family sessions.

FAMILY VALUES

1 A family is not a family without children

2 A family is a group of people with the same surname

3 Families are something that everyone has

4 You have to be related to be a family

5 Families should do things together

6 Christmas is a special time for families

7 Fathers are the head of the household

8 A family has a mum, a dad and children

9 To be a family you have to live together

10 You always love your family

11 Parents have all the power in families

12 Children should be allowed to choose who they live with if their parents split up

13 Step families are never happy

14 You only have one mum

15 Grandparents are important members of a family

16 Parents always have favourites

17 Families should have pets

18 You shouldn't have to pay to live with your family

19 Parents should be responsible for what their children do

43 PICTURE PARENTS

This explores the role of mothers and fathers and how they are shown in the media. If you are working with a large number of young people, ask them to form smaller groups of no more than six for this activity.

AIM

To encourage discussion around how parents are depicted in newspapers and magazines and produce an advert for parenthood.

YOU WILL NEED

- Large sheets of paper
- Glue
- Scissors
- Magazines (ones that are likely to show parents and children)
- Newspapers
- Marker pens

HOW TO DO IT

Equip each group with glue, scissors and marker pens. As you hand out the magazines and newspapers explain that you are setting each group the task of using collage to produce an advert that reflects how parents are depicted in the media.

Ask one group to produce an advert for fatherhood and the other to devise one for motherhood. Explain that they can use the markers to add speech bubbles or words.

Allow 20 minutes to half-an-hour for the groups to complete their collage.

Once they have finished ask the young people to clear away the materials and display their advert.

Encourage each group to feed back what they have put together. Facilitate any discussion points raised. Are mothers and fathers shown in the same way? Is parenthood portrayed as a positive or negative thing? How easy was it to find images of fathers? Are mixed heritage families represented? What about parents with disabilities?

Conclude by asking the group to consider if they think that the media's representation is a true reflection of most people's experience of having children. Facilitate a discussion around the answers given.

44 YOU'RE LATE!

This provides the opportunity for young people to re-write a typical scenario the way they think it should be! Depending on how big your group is you can do a storyboard for as many characters as you like that shows the different perspectives when a young person returns home late – again!

AIM

To encourage young people to think of the consequences of returning home late and the impact this has on different family members.

YOU WILL NEED

- A storyboard sheet for each group
- Pens

HOW TO DO IT

Read out the following scenario to the whole group.

'You are coming home after a night out with friends. You are over two hours late, and know you are going to be in big trouble when you do get home. You promised your mum you would be in by 10.00pm. as it is a school night, but you ended up going to a club with a mate. The problem is that as well as being late you also promised not to go to the club as it has a bad reputation and your family don't approve ...'

In groups of three or four using the storyboard sheet ask the young people to construct a comic strip which shows what happens next.

Give each group the task of telling the story from a different character's point of view:

- the young person;
- the mum or dad;
- the young person's friend; and
- another member of the family.

Encourage the groups to think about the consequences of actions, what they could have done differently and what could be done to resolve the conflict.

YOU'RE LATE

Use the storyboard to show what happens next ...

45 WHAT THEY THINK OF ME

This only really works in very small groups or with individuals. You need to have built a good relationship with the young people as you are asking them to reflect on very personal issues.

AIM

To gain an understanding of how the young person thinks they are perceived by their family and to open up discussions about family life.

YOU WILL NEED

- Copies of the 'What they think of me' sheet
- Pens

HOW TO DO IT

Begin by making sure that the young people you plan to work with are sure about the boundaries of your confidentiality. They need to be clear that there are some things you would need to share with the appropriate agencies which offers them the choice to disclose or not.

Explain that you are asking them to reflect on what they think different members of their family would say about them if asked. Ask them to think about both positive and maybe not so good points. For example, 'my mum thinks that I am a pain because I don't make my bed, but she would also say I am a good laugh because she likes my jokes!'.

Hand out the sheet and allow about ten minutes for the young people to consider how they think they are seen. Encourage them to reflect on life at home in general and not just to focus on the last row they had or the bits that annoy them most!

Ask them to share what they feel comfortable with. Are there similarities or themes? Are the comments made fair? What could be done towards changing some of the negative points? Are the good parts always adequately recognised? How do these thoughts compare with what they would like to be said about them?

Close the discussion by asking each member of the group to say something positive about each of the people they have mentioned on their sheet.

WHAT THEY THINK OF ME!

Mum thinks ...

Dad thinks ...

My brother/sister thinks ...

Grandparents think ...

Other people important to me think ...

I think this because ...

46 RULES OF THE HOUSE

This exercise works on the basis that wherever you live there are 'rules'. If you live at home your parents usually set these, but renting or flat sharing has its own set of rules that the group may not have considered!

AIM

The main aim of taking part in this session is to enable young people to share experiences and discuss potential areas of conflict. By acknowledging that these may be different depending on where and who you live with the young people can begin to develop strategies to negotiate or accept them.

YOU WILL NEED

- Post-it pads
- Pens
- Contact numbers for local support groups and social services

HOW TO DO IT

Begin the session with a conversation about what home means. Is it just a place to sleep and store your clothes? Does it mean more? Why?

Then hand out the Post-it notes and pens. Ask the group to individually consider the conversation that they have just had and focus on the good and bad parts of living with parents/carers.

When they have thought about it, ask the young people to use three Post-it notes to write:

- the five best things about living at home;
- the five worst things about living at home; and
- five things that they would do differently if they left home.

Once the group has completed the task ask them to stick their notes in three separate piles. They do not have to put their names on them.

Ask for a volunteer from the group to read out the best things. Are there similarities? For example, how many said 'I get my washing done'. Discuss this and encourage group members to enlarge upon what they have said.

Invite another volunteer to go through the same process with the worst things. These are usually the rules of the house as in 'while you live under my roof ...' and are often the cause of real tension in the home. What are the major areas of conflict? Be sensitive to

the fact that you may be asking the group to share experiences they find difficult or painful to talk about. Make sure that you have the numbers of ChildLine, social services or your local youth counselling centre and that you have explained the boundaries of your confidentiality. It is also a good idea to have information about the legalities regarding young people living away from home, including those in the care of the local authority.

Then look at the pile of things that would be done differently. Review in the same way as the other notes, but additionally challenge or question the practicalities involved in achieving the wish list. For example, how realistic is it to say 'I would play my music as loud as I want, whenever I want ...'. Question if this would be possible, unless they are planning to live on an uninhabited desert island!

Invite the group to look again at the wish list and discuss if there is any way that a compromise could be worked towards which would enable them to remove some of the worst things and add to the best list. For example, for the young person who gets told off for coming in late at night this could be a type of contract between them and their parent that they will phone if they are going to be late.

Dependent on how much of an issue this is for the group you can work through each of the negative points and see how they could be re-framed to become more acceptable to the young person and their parent.

Agree with the group to each work on one area raised during the session for the next week and suggest that you review how the tactics worked (or didn't!) when you meet again.

47 SNOWSTORM

To make this work you need to support the young people to work quickly and to go with their first ideas.

AIM

To facilitate a brain storming session around family relationships.

YOU WILL NEED

- Post-it notes
- Pens
- A watch

HOW TO DO IT

Before the young people arrive clear a space on the wall or cover an area with large sheets of coloured paper.

Hand out wads of Post-it notes and a pen to each person in the group.

Now, set the group the task of quickly thinking what words spring to mind if you say the word family! Then ask them to write the words on the Post-it notes and stick them onto the wall space. Set a time limit to contain the activity and encourage first thoughts only.

Ask the group to be as open as they feel comfortable with - including good and bad things!

Agree that no-one in the group can move a sticker once it has been placed at this point whether they agree or disagree with what it says.

Once all the Post-its are in place ask the group to stand back and look at the snowstorm it has created.

Now ask the young people to go up to the wall in turn and start to group the words. So, for example, all the notes that say 'safe' or similar go together as do all the 'rules' and 'arguments'.

Review the wall as a whole group. What are the main issues emerging? Pull out a few of the major groupings and discuss further.

From this you should be able to identify any areas for further sessions.

48 PARENT POWER

These examples of parental responsibility are intended as conversation starters. Smaller groups that you know well are more effective because everyone has a better opportunity to contribute and you are more likely to be aware of issues raised that may be sensitive.

AIM

To offer information to young people that promotes discussion and debate over the roles and responsibilities of parents.

YOU WILL NEED

- The 'Parent power' sheet (which gives you the answers!)
- Additional leaflets and contact numbers for those experiencing difficulties at home

HOW TO DO IT

In preparation for the session make sure that you have plenty of comfy chairs grouped together to provide a good setting for relaxed conversation. If you have a chill out area in your club use this, or perhaps see if you can dim the lighting and use candles.

Once the young people are seated begin the session by agreeing some groundrules. These may include:

- that no-one can enter the group once the discussion has started;
- information shared stays within the group (apart from child protection concerns); and
- no-one speaks over someone else.

Explain the aim of the session and begin to read out one of the statements on the 'Parent power' sheet. It does not matter how many you get through or what order you read them out in - it may be best to start with something that you know the group will feel strongly about to start a good debate!

After each statement ask questions to encourage discussion. For example, do they think this is fair? Who has the right to make decisions for a young person? Do parents take up these responsibilities? Do parents have more or less power that the group thought? Are they happy for their parents to make decisions for them?

Finally, ask the group to consider positive ways that they can help inform their parents and so negotiate decisions that they are happy with.

PARENT POWER

1 **It is your parents' responsibility to make sure you get to school every day.**
True - parents have the main responsibility to ensure that their child is educated. The 1996 Education Act makes it compulsory for young people between the ages of 5 and 16 to go to school, and their parents' duty to get them there. The only exception to this is if your parents decide to educate you at home and then the local authority has to make sure it is appropriate. So, if you don't go to school your parents can be taken to court.

2 **At 18 you are still in the custody and care of your parents and you have to ask their permission to leave home.**
True - but realistically courts are not likely to make anyone over the age of 16 return home if they are able to provide themselves with somewhere to live and are not at risk of harm.

3 **At 16 you can marry and young women can lawfully have sex, but your parents have the right to stop you taking part in sex education lessons at school if they want to.**
True - but only the bits that are not part of the national curriculum. The 1993 Education Act says that all young people must have appropriate sex education at school, but your parents can refuse to let you take part in anything they object to.

4 **You can change your name any time you want, although to do it properly you need a change of name deed which a solicitor can help you with.**
False - over 18 you can call yourself what you like with a deed, before then you cannot do it without the agreement of both parents and a deed. If they won't both agree it could go to court for the court to decide.

5 **It is illegal for parents to smack their children.**
False - not at the moment! Parents have the right to discipline their children and this can include smacking. It is illegal in some countries though, for example, Austria, Sweden and Cyprus.

6 **You do not need your parents' consent for medical or dental treatment if you are 16.**
True - if you are 16 or over you do not need your parents' permission to accept or refuse treatment.

7 **If you are charged with an offence and go to court your parents have to go with you.**
True - if you are under 16, but they only have to go if they are ordered to if you are 16 or 17.

Source: *Young Citizens Passport 1999/2000*

49 THE FLATMATE FROM HELL

The idea of this activity is to ask the group you are working with what attributes they most fear in a potential flatmate. It works well with young people who are contemplating leaving home or struggling with house rules imposed by parents. It can be used effectively with the following session (50), which looks at the practicalities of affording your own place.

AIM

The aim of the session is to open up discussion with a group around the pros and potential cons of independent living and flat sharing.

YOU WILL NEED

- Markers
- Flipchart paper and stands

HOW TO DO IT

With your co-worker set up two flipchart stands. Using a different colour fluorescent pen for each stand draw a rough outline of a human figure. Head one sheet 'desirable' and the other 'undesirable'.

Gather the group together so that everyone can see the flipcharts. Ask the group to nominate two young people to write up responses to the questions that you are going to ask.

First, ask the group to think of all the attributes that would make someone the 'flatmate from hell'. As they call their ideas out a volunteer notes down the suggestions. This can range from something like smoking to leaving the toilet seat up, to borrowing clothes without asking to making lots of noise when they come home late!

Then, do a similar exercise looking at all the personal qualities that would make a person 'ideal' and easy and comfortable to live with. Suggestions for the perfect partner could be clean, tidy and generous with cash or a good cook.

The session should be fun. Encourage the group to be as creative as they like and put everything down.

Once the lists are up and the group has had a chance to consider what everybody has contributed ask them to form a circle. Facilitate a discussion that explores how they see themselves (realistically) on a scale from one flatmate description to the other.

Now ask the group to look at how this might be reflected back at home living with parents and being more like reasonable flatmates rather than 'nightmare teenagers'. Are things that they listed on their flatmate from hell similar to issues that cause arguments at home? What changes could be made, on both sides, to make things less tense? How could compromises be made? Agree strategies and action plans to try out for a week and review with the young people at next week's session.

50 THE COST OF LIVING

This works well with small groups aged 14+ who have already done some work around independent living and leaving home.

AIM

To encourage young people to look at the financial implications of setting up their own home.

YOU WILL NEED

- Property pages from local newspapers
- Information about council tax from your local housing department or council
- Information and figures for benefit entitlements for under 21s.
- Information and figures on average wages for under 21s
- Leaflets on benefits for young people and any local youth housing project
- Calculators
- Pens
- Copies of the 'Cost of living' sheet

HOW TO DO IT

Before you begin the session ask the young people to share how much they currently pay their parents/carers to live at home. If this is nothing, ask if they have older siblings who pay or friends who make a contribution.

Facilitate a short discussion around how the group feels about paying money to live at home, what they think it pays for and if this is discussed with them in any detail.

Then, working in a circle so everyone can see each other, hand out the property pages that you have collected from your local papers. Ask the young people to look particularly at the flats and single rooms for rent. Encourage the group to look at landlord's requirements, for example, a month's rent in advance or a deposit. Do most accept DHSS benefits? Is there an age or gender requirement stipulated?

When the group has had a chance to get an idea of what sort of accommodation is available for young people, hand out the 'Cost of living' sheets. Make the information on council tax available.

Ask the young people independently or in pairs to prepare a budget sheet for a typical month if they left home and rented one of the properties advertised. Encourage them to be as honest as possible about how much they would usually spend on going out and clothes, for example. Stress that a social life is important for most people and that adults would be encouraged to include this too when planning to set up home. Hand out calculators so that they can arrive at a grand total.

When everyone has completed their sheet gather the group back into a circle. Ask for feedback from the process. What are the costs like? Are the totals similar? Is it more or less than what they thought? What is the most expensive part of living away from home?

Finally, hand out information about the benefits that young people are entitled to, and the average wages for under 21s.

In pairs ask the group to look at the total on their sheet and compare this to the average income for a young person. Does it add up? What is the difference? Could they manage?

Review the session and learning outcomes. Agree with the group any further sessions to explore issues that have been raised in more depth.

COST OF LIVING

Have a look at the grid below and complete the sections based on the information you have and what you currently spend. This should cover a typical month. If there are sections you are not sure of make a guess, but put something in each box.

	£
RENT	
COUNCIL TAX	
HEATING AND LIGHTING (may be included in rent)	
TELEPHONE	
FOOD AND DRINK	
HOUSEHOLD GOODS (light bulbs, toilet rolls, etc)	
CLOTHES	
GOING OUT and RECREATION	
EXTRAS (CDs, presents, toiletries, etc)	
TOTAL	

51 FAMILY MAP

You can do this exercise with young people individually or in small groups. The main point to the activity is to acknowledge that all families are different; they come in lots of different shapes and sizes - all are valid.

AIM

To acknowledge that all families are different and should be valued equally, and to share and discuss the range of cultures and traditions in the group.

YOU WILL NEED

- Flipchart paper
- Pens
- Marker pens

HOW TO DO IT

Hand out sheets of flipchart paper to each young person and make a good selection of marker pens available.

Explain that what you want the group to do is to draw a family map that shows the people, things and traditions that are important to their family and make it what it is. This should be done individually with an opportunity to share later. If you know that you have a number of young people in the group who have difficulties in writing set the activity as a drawing task for everyone.

Ask the group to think about their family in the broadest sense - not just their parents or siblings but other people that make a contribution to the way their family is. This can include family friends, cousins, step-relations or childminders, grandparents, etc - in fact anyone who is important to them should be on it! You could demonstrate by making a map of your own family if you think that this will help start the group off. Stress that the drawings can be as simple as they like - you are not expecting portraits!

Once the important people are 'mapped', ask the group to think about traditions and celebrations that are important. This could be religious celebrations such as Midnight Mass at Christmas, Ramadan or Diwali or family rituals such as Sunday lunch or a weekly visit to grandparents. Once again encourage the young people to think about things that have always happened in their home lives. Make sure you are sensitive to the needs of the group - this could be a painful experience for some members.

Finally, ask the group to mark out important events that happen or have happened. Examples for this may be things such as a parent's wedding or the birth of a younger sibling or a special family holiday.

Once all the maps are complete ask the group to come together. Offer the young people the opportunity to share family maps - if this is not appropriate ask them to share some of the things they have recorded. Are there similarities? What expectations are there from parents/carers to maintain these traditions?

Facilitate a discussion about how family expectations change (or don't) as the group have grown up. Are these realistic? Look at ways that tension could be reduced or expectations questioned effectively.

52 ACT OUT FAMILIES!

This activity aims to work through a range of family situations. The cards are non-prescriptive so the young people can choose who they represent. It should be played at a fairly fast pace so that everybody has the chance to act out a character.

AIM

To introduce the group to role-play and drama-based activities. It also enables group members to act out issues which may be relevant to them in a safe environment.

YOU WILL NEED

- A copy of the set of 'Act out families' cards
- Information around issues likely to be raised in the session

HOW TO DO IT

Start the session with a short discussion about how non-verbal communication often shows others how we are feeling or behaving without any words being spoken. Suggest this is true for all people including parents and families. Ask the young people to consider this and to think about their own body language.

Next, explain that you are going to ask for two volunteers to demonstrate this. Introduce the set of cards you have and the game. Tell the group that one person will act out what is on the card, in any role they choose, e.g. a mother or sister. The other will play the role of a young person returning home and should ask questions to try and guess what is on the card. All questions must be answered in character so, for example, if your card says 'being angry', you can reply to the question 'How are you?' by shouting, 'What time do you call this?'.

If you are met with a shy silence, volunteer yourself and your co-worker to take the first turn. Often this is a great success, especially if you really over act!

A guess can be made at any stage in the process. If it is correct the young person takes a new card and acts out the next role. A new volunteer comes forward to play the young person returning home and tries to guess what they are acting out. If the guess is wrong continue until they get it right.

This should be a game that is thought provoking, but good fun. Be aware that some cards may be uncomfortable for the young person who draws it to act out. For example, if you are aware that a young person has recently had a huge argument with her father it may be inappropriate to ask her to act out a similar situation. You will need to be sensitive to the group's needs and if necessary swap cards.

ACT OUT FAMILIES CARDS

Being ignored	Being listened to	Being lied to	Being a liar
Being scared	Being a bully	Being bullied	Being happy
Being upset	Being proud	Being in love	Being lonely
Being nosy	Being rich	Being poor	Being kind
Being excited	Being bored	Being tired	Being silly
Being angry	Being worried	Being disappointed	Being frustrated

53 TIMELINES

The idea of this exercise is to develop a 'family timeline' with the group that shows the progress of a young person through to adulthood. It allows the young people to explore issues and major events in a non-personal way, as the timeline is not exclusive to any one individual. However, you could make it person specific for one-to-one work if you needed to.

AIM

To encourage the young people to think about important milestones in the life of a family and how this impacts on the different members.

YOU WILL NEED

- Flipchart paper taped together to make the timeline for the wall
- Marker pens

HOW TO DO IT

Before the group arrives prepare the timeline by taping flipchart sheets end-to-end together along a large stretch of wall. Make sure this is set at a height that all members of your group can reach it comfortably, including any wheelchair users.

With a thick black marker write the words 'BIRTH' at the start of your timeline and 'ADULTHOOD' at the end.

Once your group has settled explain what the aim of the timeline is and what you are trying to produce together.

Invite the young people one at a time to take a pen and write important landmarks in the appropriate place on the timeline. This should include any event or change that has an impact. For example, a child starting school or moving house or parents divorcing. Encourage the group to include religious celebrations and rites of passage such as Confirmation and Barmitzvah. Also map physical changes such as puberty, starting to shave and the onset of menstruation. As this is not one person's timeline it is fine to include all of these on the one sheet.

Once the timeline is complete encourage the young people to stand back and look at what has been produced. Are there definite stages of development? Are there specific markers towards adulthood within some cultures? Are there gender specific milestones? How do relationships within families change as children grow to maturity? You might want to debate with the group what age they consider adulthood to be and what defines it.

54 SHIELDS

Shields can be used in small group situations for all ages or as part of a one-to-one session. It is a good way of encouraging young people with poor literacy skills to take part as you can decide to make it pictorial only. A variation would be to do the exercise as a collage using pictures from magazines.

AIM

To encourage young people to reflect on the relationships within their family in the past, now and how they would like them to be in the future.

YOU WILL NEED

- Flipchart paper
- Lots of coloured markers and pens

HOW TO DO IT

Give the young people a sheet of paper and ask them to choose some pens to work with.

Take a sheet for yourself and draw a large shield shape in the middle. Ask the group to do the same. Explain that this is not a test of how well they draw and that they do not have to all produce the same shaped shield.

Once everyone has a shield ask him or her to divide it into three equal areas. Once again demonstrate this on yours.

Explain that each third will represent a part of their life. One is the past and should show what has happened in their family to date. This includes their relationships with parents, carers and siblings as well as where they live and what they do. The second is the present showing what is going on for them now, and the third is the future.

The present should focus on how it is to live at home now that they are young adults. Are the same people close to them? Are there new family members to build relationships with? Are the same things important? Ask them to put a star by things and people that appear in both parts.

The future can show all their hopes, ambitions and dreams. Ask them where they see themselves in 15 years time. What kind of relationship do they think they will have with their family? Is there an older brother or sister who is a role model for life after leaving home? Do they want to change things? Once again ask the group to star people that are in all three sections.

The depth of the information on the shields will vary depending on how well you know the young people, but it is always good to draw up some kind of agreement around confidentiality before you start.

When everyone has completed their shield bring the group back together and form a circle. Each person then shares the parts they feel comfortable with. Draw out similarities and discuss ideas.

You can take this further and look at action plans for achievable goals.

55 TWO SIDES

This drama-based activity works on the old theory that there are two sides to every story. It works best with small groups of young people aged 14+ who may have similar experiences to those depicted.

AIM

This role play encourages young people to work through an issue from two different viewpoints, hopefully reaching a compromise and resolving potential conflict.

YOU WILL NEED

- A set of the 'Two sides' cards

HOW TO DO IT

Introduce the session and ask the young people to choose a partner to work with.

Hand a corresponding card to each couple, asking that they do not share what is written on it. This is important, as there is a tendency to second guess what is going to be said rather than working through the role play together.

You can set a time limit on the activity so that the young people feel that there are some boundaries – 20 minutes is usually enough, but you can agree this with your group.

Ask each pair to go and find a space to work through the situation on their cards. Encourage them to reach a resolution that they can share when the group comes back together.

Once everyone is ready form a circle and share the process. Ask each pair to outline their situation and how they worked with it. Make sure you tell the group that they only need share what they are comfortable with. Facilitate the feedback by asking questions about how it felt to be the parent as well as the child. How easy was it to resolve conflict? How quickly was compromise reached?

TWO SIDES

1a You want your ears pierced – your mum has said 'no', how are you going to convince her to change her mind?

1b Your daughter wants her ears pierced – you have said 'no', you had yours done when you were her age and they went septic. You don't want that to happen to your child.

2a You are going to your friend's party. Your dad has said 'yes' but wants you home by 11.30pm. Everyone else is allowed to stay later, what are you going to say?

2b Your son is going to his friend's party. You have no problem with this but you are worried about him walking home late at night – there might be trouble...

3a Your mum wants you to babysit for your little brother – again. You want to go out with your mate, how can you explain?

3b You need to go to work, they are looking to make redundancies and you don't want to give them an excuse for it to be you! You don't like asking again but what else can you do?

4a You have decided to give up eating meat. You think it is really cruel to kill animals but your family laugh and say it is just a phase, how can you make them see how important this is to you?

4b Yesterday you cooked a huge family meal. As you dish it up your daughter announces that she is now a vegetarian! How inconsiderate! Doesn't she know how long it took you to prepare this?

5a You have seen some new trainers that you must have in town. You have asked your mum, but she just said you had to make do with your old ones – why can't she understand?

5b Your son has asked for new trainers. They are far more than you can afford but he just keeps on asking ...

56 FAMILY FEUDS

You will need to be sensitive to the fact that some of the young people in the group may have experienced some of the situations discussed in this exploration of family conflict.

AIM

To encourage young people to reflect on what leads to family conflict and breakdown.

YOU WILL NEED

- Post-it notes
- Pens

HOW TO DO IT

In groups of up to eight young people, explain that this activity aims to explore some of the issues that lead to arguments and break ups in families.

Hand out two Post-it notes and a pen to each member of the group.

Ask the young people to write a different situation or issue that they think causes tensions at home. Stress that you are not asking the group to share personal experiences and that this does not have to be something that has happened to them. Some examples you could suggest are coming home late, not making beds, running up huge phone bills or not liking a parent's new partner.

As they finish ask the young people to stick their suggestions in the middle of the circle.

Now, encourage the group to review what has been written. Ask the young people to reflect on the different ideas and together begin to rank them in order of what issues they think will damage family relationships. Promote discussion around each point raised.

Now review the process. How easy was it to rank the Post-it notes? Were there themes or similarities that aided the process? Were there any gender issues? How does religion or culture affect parents' perception of what is OK or not?

LOVE, SEX AND ALL THAT ...

57 RELATIONSHIP GRID

This activity can be used as a way of encouraging young people to think about what constitutes an appropriate relationship. It can be used successfully in either mixed gender or single-sex groups because the idea is to promote discussion rather than focus on anything too personal.

AIM

To look at the different types of relationships that we have with people in our lives, and consider what makes a relationship 'appropriate' or not.

YOU WILL NEED

- A copy of the "Relationship grid' for each member of the group

HOW TO DO IT

Hand out copies of the grid and introduce the session. Ask the group to consider the different types of relationships they have with all the people involved in their lives. Explain the three headings on the relationship grid - social, friendship and intimate. Suggest that some relationships may belong in different areas on the grid at different stages in the relationship. For example, a boyfriend may be met socially, become a friend and then later a partner.

Read through the list of potential people that a young person may know or have a relationship with and ask them to categorise them on the grid. Ask that the young people do this individually to begin with, but inform them that you will be asking them to share something they feel comfortable with at the end.

Facilitate a discussion around the different types of relationships we all have, including any disagreements within the group.

- Teacher
- Doctor
- Mother
- Youth worker
- Father
- Cousin
- Uncle
- Babysitter
- Husband
- Girlfriend
- Sister
- Employer
- Sports coach
- Brother
- Milkman
- Priest
- Best mate
- Boyfriend
- Wife
- Social worker
- Friend's parent
- Bus driver
- Shop assistant

RELATIONSHIP GRID

Social	Friendship	Intimate

58 ON A SCALE OF ...

The idea of this activity is to get young people thinking about their own values and those of their peers. You can do it in either mixed gender or single-sex groups of up to eight young people. If you are working with a larger group you could use two sets of cards and invite them to share and compare answers.

AIM

The aim of the session is to open up a discussion around personal values.

YOU WILL NEED

- A set of the cards depicting situations
- A card marked 'acceptable' and a card marked 'unacceptable' in a different colour to the other cards

HOW TO DO IT

Hand out the set of situation cards to the group and ask them to read each of the situations offered.

Mark two opposing poles on the floor with the 'acceptable' and 'unacceptable' cards. Explain that what you want the young people to do is to rate the cards as acceptable, i.e. normal or unacceptable, i.e. unusual behaviour. Stress that there is not always a right or wrong answer, many responses are based on cultural or social acceptance, which may differ within the group.

Once they have placed the cards in a line between the poles, ask the group to sit back and look at where they have been positioned.

Is everyone in agreement? Invite the young people to change the position of any card they disagree with, explaining why as they do it. If the group are shy to do this you could start by questioning why a particular card is placed where it is and start the discussions from there.

ON A SCALE OF ...

A man kissing a woman in the street	A young couple snogging in public
An elderly couple holding hands as they walk along	A young woman slapping her boyfriend
A young man hitting his girlfriend	A young man kissing his friend's girlfriend
A man swearing at his girlfriend in public	Shouting abuse down the phone
A gay couple cuddling at a party	A lesbian couple holding hands in the cinema
A young man crying	A young man telling his friends that he has had sex with his girlfriend
A woman crying	A young woman telling her friends that she has slept with her boyfriend
A couple having sex in a car after dark in a public place	A young man lying about losing his virginity
Thinking a girl means 'yes' when she says 'no'	A young woman lying about who she has slept with
A woman hitting a woman	A young couple having sex at a party while drunk

59 HOW SAFE IS SAFE?

This activity can be done with up to six young people. You will need to have built a good relationship with the young people for them to feel comfortable in participating. A leaflet introducing the topics that may be covered during the session should be sent home to parents/carers to inform them. You will also need to be sensitive to the groups' age and cultural background. It works well with single-sex groups where the young people may feel more confident in asking questions and discussing issues raised.

AIM

To look at what is meant by safe sex in a confidential and supportive group. Leaflets and information about sexually transmitted diseases and contraceptives can support this. The session forms part of an ongoing sex education programme and is a good way of opening discussions around sexual health issues and choices.

YOU WILL NEED

- Small post-it notes
- Pens
- Two A4 sheets of brightly coloured paper
- Sexual health leaflets

HOW TO DO IT

On the two coloured sheets of paper write the words 'safe' and 'less safe' and place them about two metres apart on the floor.

Give each member of the group a pen and three Post-it notes. If you have a small group hand out more Post-it pads. Ask the young people to write on their paper a sexual act. Explain that they should do this individually and not show each other yet. Stress that you are not asking if they have done what they write down and that nobody will be questioned about their experiences.

When each young person has completed the task ask him or her to take turns to place a paper between the 'safe' and 'less safe' poles. Once this has been done ask the group to consider if they feel all the papers are in the right place. They can then discuss with each other and agree a final sequence. For example, kissing should appear very close to 'safe' whereas unprotected sex will be close to the 'less safe' area.

60 BACK OFF!

This session works well as part of a positive relationship programme. I have used it with young women that I have met over several weeks and who have begun to discuss issues freely in a group.

AIM

To encourage young women to look at situations and make risk assessments. It also provides a framework for keeping safe and looks at ways to be assertive in situations that may not feel comfortable.

YOU WILL NEED

- A copy of the work sheet, enlarged and cut out
- 2 x sheets of coloured paper, marked 'Ok' and 'Back off'
- Blu-tack

HOW TO DO IT

Place the sheet marked 'Ok' on the ground and the other sheet marked 'Back off' about two metres apart. Use Blu-tack if it is windy!

Hand out the situations marked A to L. Ask the young women to place them between the two sheets of paper where they feel that they should be positioned. Explain the 'Ok' is where they feel most comfortable, 'Back off' is unacceptable and any they are not sure of should go in the middle. If there is any disagreement, ask the young women to comment and discuss.

For those that the group feels are unacceptable suggest ways that the young women could make their feelings understood and how to assert themselves.

For any in the middle encourage discussion until the group can agree.

BACK OFF!

A A stranger asks you for directions from his car

B A youth worker asks to meet you outside of youth club hours

C A family friend asks you for a kiss at a family party

D A boy at school/college makes remarks about the size of your breasts

E You are walking home at night alone and think that someone is behind you

F Someone rings your mobile and makes suggestive remarks down the phone

G A workman wolf whistles at you from a building site

H A girl from school/college shouts insults at you in the street

I An older boy you meet at a club offers to walk you home

J A man touches you on the train

K A male teacher comments how nice you look in a skirt

L You are at a party and a boy starts dancing very close to you and pressing himself against you

61 WHAT HAPPENS NEXT?

This can be used as part of a programme around self-esteem and positive personal relationships. Basically, it offers a scenario and asks the question what happens next? to each of the characters.

AIM

To encourage the young people to look at a set of circumstances from different perspectives and to encourage discussion around love, trust and friendship.

YOU WILL NEED

- Copies of Jodie's story

HOW TO DO IT

Introduce the session by explaining to the group that they will be looking at a scenario involving two young people and their friends. Stress that what you want the group to do is to consider what they think will happen next, and what effect each character's actions will have on each other, themselves and the group.

Split the group into twos or threes and hand them a copy of the scenario to study. If you know that you have a high number of young people who find reading a problem, read the scenario to the whole group before dividing them up.

Ask each smaller group to consider the feelings, actions and potential choices for either Jodie or Dean. They can choose this themselves or you can set the group a role to look at.

Allow about 15 minutes for discussion and then bring the group back together. Ask each group to feedback the main points that they have made and facilitate a discussion around issues raised.

JODIE'S STORY

Jodie is 16 and very shy. She lives with her mum and her stepfather who she hates as she thinks that he is the reason her dad left home.

Jodie is friendly with the young people at the youth centre, although she is quiet and tends to hang about on her own. She has told the other young women that she really fancies Dean and spends much of her time drawing and decorating hearts with his name and hers entwined.

Dean is slightly older than the rest of the group and well liked by everyone for his good sense of humour and outgoing personality. He used to live in London and still remains in contact with some of his London friends. He often recounts stories of his exciting social life in the city, including a number of ex-girlfriends, and boasts frequently about the number of sexual partners he has had. Dean is enjoying the additional status that Jodie's attention has given him with the other young men as Jodie is considered very good looking.

Dean and Jodie finally get together at a party and become boy/girlfriend. During the next few evenings Dean tells his mates every intimate detail of the time he has spent with Jodie. Jodie does not take part in these conversations herself, but does not appear to object to the group knowing about their growing relationship.

Tonight, Jodie is talking enthusiastically with a female youth worker and the other young women about how happy she is to be with Dean. She explains that this is the first time that she has found a male she can trust, and that she does not want to lose him.

Upstairs, Dean is sitting on the floor with three other young men. Dean is loudly describing what has taken place with Jodie since they last met. The young men listen closely and make suggestive gestures with their hands. Dean begins loudly telling the young men that he is planning to take up photography, particularly pornographic photographs of Jodie. He says that for a fee he will share these with them and asks for requests of what they would most like to see. Suddenly Jodie opens the door with the group of young women behind her. It is obvious to everyone in the room that all the female members of the group have overheard the conversation.

Jodie pushes past her friends in tears and runs out into the night.

62 WHAT DID YOU CALL ME?

This activity is a good prelude to work around young gay and lesbian issues. As with any anti-oppressive practice sessions you will need to be sensitive to the dynamics of the group to ensure that you are not creating a situation that excludes or isolates any member.

AIM

To explore the attitudes and prejudice experienced by young gays and lesbians and provoke discussion around perceptions and reality.

YOU WILL NEED

- Flipchart paper
- Marker pens
- Information about local gay and lesbian groups and contact numbers for local and national support/information groups
- An understanding of the legal implications for gay relationships

HOW TO DO IT

Gather the young people together in a circle or group where they can see and hear each other and you. Introduce the session and the aim of the activity.

Ask for two volunteers to scribe and seat them on either side of you with a flipchart sheet and different colour markers.

Next, ask the group to think of all the slang names and expressions that they have heard to describe gay and lesbian people. Stress that you are not asking if they have ever called somebody this, or inviting them to share information about their own sexual orientation. You may want to develop this so that the young people also share who they have heard use the term. For example, 'My dad always calls gay men poofs'. This can be explored later.

Record all the names for gay men on one sheet and lesbian women on the other.

You will find that there are far more names and terms of abuse for gay men than for lesbians. Ask the group to consider why they think this is and facilitate a discussion around the findings. Bring into this the legalities for gay sex. What are the stereotypes that have been created, for example, butch lesbians? How true are they?

63 GRAFFITI WALL

This is a good way to start a session around relationships. You can tailor the subject of the graffiti to fit with what you have planned for the group.

AIM

To begin a dialogue around relationships and what they mean to the group.

YOU WILL NEED

- A large wall or noticeboard
- Flipchart sheets
- Marker pens

HOW TO DO IT

Cover a large area of wall with flipchart paper before the young people arrive.

Choose a specific theme, for example:

- Why do people get married?
- What do you want in your ideal partner?
- Why do relationships break up?

Write your question along the top of the graffiti sheet to focus the group.

When the young people arrive ask them the question, show them the pens – and stand well back!

Explain that no-one has the right to alter or erase someone else's comments – there will be space to challenge at the end. If they see anything they especially agree with ask them to put a tick by the comment or word.

Ensure that everybody has a go at expressing themselves and that no-one takes over the wall.

Once the space has been filled ask the group to stand back and review what they have produced. Are there common themes? How many ticks are there? Does anyone want to talk about what they have written or ask about anything put on the wall?

64 DEAR AGONY UNCLE ...

This opens up discussions around personal issues in a way that most young people are familiar with in magazines. It gives them the opportunity to play agony aunt or uncle and solve the problems!

AIM

To involve young people in the solutions to dilemmas and issues in a non-personal way.

YOU WILL NEED

- Copies of the 'Dear agony uncle' sheets

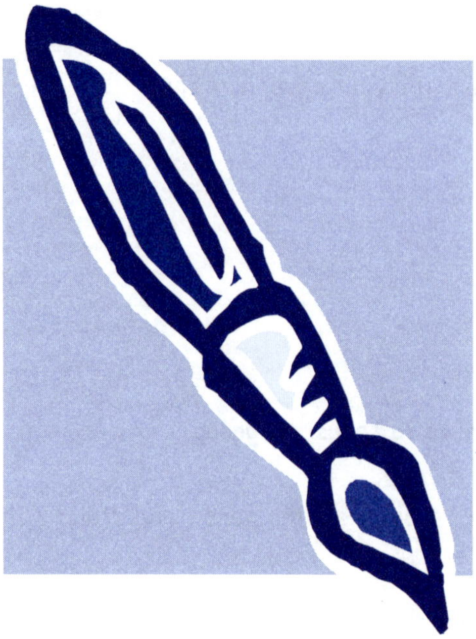

HOW TO DO IT

Explain to the young people what the aims of the sessions are and divide them into smaller groups. You can do this as a mixed gender activity or you may decide that the young people will get more out of their discussions if they work in single-sex groups.

Hand each small group a 'Dear agony uncle' sheet and ask for a volunteer to read the letter to the other young people in their group. Stress that all characters and situations are fictional and certainly do not relate to anyone in the group. This should stop everyone trying to guess whose problem they are really discussing!

Once the young people have their problem to look at ask them to discuss the situation and suggest some replies. They can either do this verbally or write a response on paper.

When everyone is happy with the advice the group is going to offer, bring the whole group back together to share problems and suggested solutions.

DEAR AGONY UNCLE ...

Dear Agony Uncle

I am 15 and really like this girl in my class. She is very popular and is always with a crowd of other girls. I know that she has had lots of boyfriends already because my best mate told me. She does smile at me when we see each other in maths, but apart from that I do not really know what she thinks of me.

I have never asked a girl out before and I really don't want to end up looking stupid, what should I do?

Warren

Dear Agony Uncle

I am 14 and have been going out with my boyfriend who is 17 for six months. I really like him, but I said I was 16 when we first met and now I am really worried because he wants us to have sex.

I am happy kissing him and messing around, but his parents are due to go away for the weekend soon and he wants me to stay over. Although he says he loves me and that he will take care of things I am really scared I will end up pregnant. I think I am too young to have sex, and my mum will go mad if she finds out.

The problem is he thinks I have done it loads of times and thinks I am going off him as I keep making excuses. Help!

Laura

Dear Agony Uncle

I am getting really worried about the fact that I don't have a girlfriend. All of my mates talk about girls all the time, but I am not really interested in girls, except as friends. I find it really hard to join in when they talk about who they fancy.

Last week we went to a party and all my mates got off with someone except me. Now they are starting to look at me when I come into the room and I heard one of the girls asking my best mate if I am gay.

I don't know what to do because I don't want all my friends to hate me, what do you think?

Dan

Dear Agony Uncle

My parents are really strict. They do not like me going out at night and want to choose my friends and who I go out with. They are very religious and expect me to be too.

The problem is that I have met a really nice boy and he has asked me to go to the youth club with him. He is my friend's brother and I met him at her house when we were doing our homework. My family only just allows me to see her, as she is not a Hindu and would be so angry if they knew what I wanted to do.

How can I explain that he is not what they think?

Rani

65 PASS THE PARCEL

This uses a familiar party game as a non-threatening method for introducing contraception and sexual health to a group. I think that this is best used with single-sex groups, as young people often feel more comfortable. You may need to obtain parental consent for young people to take part or send home leaflets outlining the session in advance.

AIM

The aim of the session is to gain a clearer understanding of the level of knowledge around contraception and sexual health within a group.

YOU WILL NEED

- A good selection of different methods of contraception
- Appropriate leaflets and contact numbers
- Newspaper or wrapping paper
- Sellotape
- Music
- Consent forms from parents to take part

HOW TO DO IT

Before the group arrives make a parcel by wrapping layers of paper interspersed with the contraceptives you have collected. Make sure you and your colleague are comfortable that you have enough information and knowledge of the contraceptives, how they work and their success rate to feel confident discussing any issues raised.

Begin the activity by gathering the young people together and asking them to sit down in a circle.

Bring out the parcel - most of the group will have played pass the parcel before, but for those who have not explain the rules.

1 As the music starts pass the parcel to the person on the left of you.
2 Continue this until the music stops.
3 Then take off the first layer of paper.
4 Name the contraceptive that you find and explain, if you can, how it works.
5 Repeat the process until all the layers are gone.

At this point you may want to set some groundrules, such as confidentiality. It is also a good idea to stress that you are not asking who has done or used what, nor do you expect the group to know all the answers.

As each contraceptive is identified add additional information, for example, the reliability of the method and whether it protects against sexually transmitted diseases.

Make sure that the whole group is included in discussions and that conversations do not become opportunities for questioning or scapegoating of individuals.

Close the session by identifying areas that the group would like to look at further.

66 RELATIONSHIP PYRAMID

The set of cards that you use for this session are non-gender specific so you can work through them with any group. However, if you have a few blank cards you can make some extras that relate to young men or women specifically.

AIM

To encourage discussion and debate about the attributes young people look for in a partner.

YOU WILL NEED

- A set of pyramid cards

HOW TO DO IT

Explain to the young people that the aim of the session is to look at what are important attributes in the people that they choose to have relationships with. Make sure that you are clear that there are no right or wrong answers for the activity – they are all down to personal priorities. It may also be useful to say that they do not have to have a specific person that they know in mind, it may be their ideal partner or just things they think they would like to find in a relationship.

Ask the young people to find a space to work together in groups of three or four. Once they are settled you can then ask them if they need to set any groundrules, for example, not to share information with the larger group unless individuals are comfortable with this.

Hand out the pyramid cards, designating someone within the group who you know is a confident reader to share what is on them with the whole group.

Now, set the task for each group to agree a pyramid of

importance for the cards. They do this by placing the least important attributes to form the base of the pyramid and building up to one card representing what they think is the most important. It should end up with five cards along the bottom row, then four, three, two and finally one at the top. Remind the group that they all have to agree the final pyramid!

If you have a small group you can do this effectively in pairs too. Give out the same explanations, but ask that one partner from each pair sets up the pyramid first and then the other reviews and alters as they see it should be. They also then have to negotiate an agreed pyramid.

Allow about 20 minutes for the pyramids to be agreed. When everyone is happy with their cards, ask the young people to place them on the floor in front of them.

Now, look at the pyramids. Are they all the same? Where there is a difference ask the group to share their thinking behind the decision as far as they are comfortable. Facilitate any discussion and encourage the young people to challenge decisions, ensuring that this does not become an opportunity for personal attacks on individual values.

Finally, ask the whole group if they can agree a pyramid of three attributes that they think are the most important for any potential partner. Remember to reinforce that this is not a trick and there are no specific answers!

Review and use to identify ongoing issues for further sessions.

RELATIONSHIP PYRAMID

Has a good body	Is a good laugh	Has lots of mates
Listens to me	Has a brain	Is good looking
Does not talk behind my back	Someone who I am proud to be with	Is not afraid to show me how they feel
Chooses to spend time with me	Does not show off to friends	Cares what I think
Makes an effort with personal hygiene	Someone I can trust	Someone my friends like

67 TOP TEN ATTRIBUTES

This looks to explore some of the myths and stereotypes around what is seen as ideal for both young men and women. It works best with mixed groups of young people aged 13+.

AIM

To offer young people the opportunity to work in single-sex groups to discuss what they think the opposite gender sees as the ideal attributes for a young woman or man. This can then be tested out in the mixed group.

YOU WILL NEED

- Flipchart paper
- Marker pens

HOW TO DO IT

Agree with the young people to work in single-sex groups for this exercise and to come back together to share and compare issues that are raised later.

Where possible the youth worker facilitating the group should be of the same gender.

Ask each group to agree a Top Ten of the attributes they think the opposite sex is looking for in a partner. So young women will be making a list of what they think young men look for in a woman and vice versa. Stress that they will all need to agree any point before it can be written up onto the group sheet. Question points raised and discuss.

Once you have a Top Ten of best points ask the group to come together to look at the sheets. Ask the groups to go through their lists, enlarging on points they have made. Then allow time for each group to be challenged or questioned about what is written. Stress that outsiders cannot change the points agreed within the groups. Support any challenges, reminding the young people that they are not being asked to judge the validity of the points made.

Look at the points made, are there any with mainly physical attributes on the lists? A balance of looks and personalities? Are there similarities between what each group thinks the other group values? How true are these? Are there any surprises? Discuss.

Bring the whole group back together and review the process.

68 MYTH OR FACT?

This tests out some well-known assumptions about sex and pregnancy and asks young people to decide if they are myth or fact. You may need to get parental consent for some young people to take part in this session.

AIM

It will give you a good understanding of the knowledge within the group around these issues and inform any further sessions.

YOU WILL NEED

- The list of statements following
- A myth card and a fact card for each young person taking part
- Appropriate leaflets and contact numbers for your local family planning clinic and GUM clinic

HOW TO DO IT

Before the young people arrive prepare for the session by setting up a circle of chairs. Make up two cards for each person using green and red cards. Write 'Myth' on all the red cards and 'Fact' on the green ones.

As the young people come in ask them to choose a place in the circle, putting yourself within the group.

Hand out a red and green card to each participant explaining what they mean.

Explain that you are going to read out a series of statements and the task is for the young people to decide if it is a myth or a fact. After each statement ask the group to raise the card that they think corresponds with the answer. Make sure that you point out that it does not matter if the young people do not know all the answers and you are not asking about personal experiences.

Be prepared to answer questions and discuss each point as it is raised. Encourage discussion and ask the group to think about other myths around sex and contraception.

MYTH OR FACT?

1 **You can't get pregnant if you do it standing up**
Myth - *if you have unprotected sex you are at risk of becoming pregnant however you do it!*

2 **You can get pregnant if you have sex during your period**
Fact - *ovulation can happen at the same time as a period so you can get pregnant.*

3 **If you go to the toilet straight after sex you won't get pregnant**
Myth - *only recognised methods of contraception protect against unwanted pregnancy. Sperm travels quickly inside the vagina to the womb so the time to take precautions is before intercourse.*

4 **If the man pulls out before he comes you don't need a condom**
Myth - *you do need a condom if you don't want to run the risk of pregnancy! Sperm can leak out of the penis before a man comes so you could get pregnant.*

5 **You can get free condoms at the family planning clinic**
Fact - *and you don't have to give your name if you are worried about this.*

6 **Condoms are a good way to protect against sexually transmitted diseases**
Fact - *condoms are the best protection from STDs.*

7 **If you use two condoms at once it is safer**
Myth - *it actually makes them less effective! Use extra-strong condoms instead.*

8 **Having sex under the age of 16 is illegal**
Fact - *the current age of consent is 16 for heterosexual partners and 18 for homosexual partners.*

9 **You can make a man ill if he has an erection and doesn't come**
Myth - *a man does not have to ejaculate every time he has an erection.*

10 **It is a good idea to use baby oil with condoms**
Myth - *it is a very bad idea! The baby oil (and any other oil-based product) can damage the condom and cause it to split.*

11 **The emergency or morning after pill only works the next morning**
Myth - *although often called the morning after pill it can actually work up to 72 hours after sex.*

12 **Only a doctor can tell you if you are pregnant**
Myth - *shop-bought pregnancy kits are very effective. However, if you think you may be pregnant you should consult your doctor.*

13 **No-one gets pregnant the first time they do it**
Myth - *once you start having periods you can get pregnant if you have penetrative sex.*

69 STATEMENTS

For this to provoke a lively, interactive debate this session is best planned for small single-sex groups of no more than four. This works well with young people you have already done some sexual health work with as you want them to be as open as possible.

AIM

To spark discussion among the group by using statements that express different opinions around moral and social opinions.

YOU WILL NEED

- The statements following

HOW TO DO IT

Prepare the area that you are going to use for the group before the young people arrive. This should be away from other groups using the club or area to avoid interruption.

Once the young people are seated, begin the session by outlining the aim and stressing that the opinions portrayed are to provoke discussion and are not representative of one person's views in particular. Make sure that you are aware of the cultural and religious diversity within the group and are sensitive to any strong feelings any of the statements may raise.

You may want to agree a contract at this point with the group. Include confidentiality and the right to challenge, but encourage the group to accept that individuals may have differing opinions and that this is okay.

Select one of the following sentences as the basis of your discussion. Read it to the young people and facilitate their conversation. Challenge or pick up on points raised to move the debate along. Is what is said correct? Is it true? Why? Are there social or cultural factors that need to be considered? Make sure that all the group have the opportunity to speak and no-one is excluded.

Close the session by reviewing what has been said and identifying any areas the group would like to explore further.

There is only one effective method of contraception and that is to say NO!

The age of consent should be raised to 18 for everyone

Boys want sex, girls want love

Disabled people shouldn't be allowed to have babies

It is wrong for gay couples to adopt children

70 AN EVENING WITH JOHNNY ...

This was a session planned for National Condom week, but could be used to raise issues on National Aids Awareness Day too. Because of the legal implications it is most appropriate for use with young people 16+ or 14+ with parental consent.

AIM

To give out correct information on the availability, range and use of condoms.

YOU WILL NEED

- Invites and consent forms
- Posters and leaflets
- Telephone numbers for local family planning clinics
- A good range of condoms
- Information about the history of condoms

HOW TO DO IT

Send out invites to the young people that you are targeting. Make sure that these look good but are clear about what you intend to cover so that they can choose to take part or not. Make sure you send out forms or information sheets to parents in advance too.

Before the session cover the walls and noticeboards of the youth centre plus any extra display boards you need with posters and information about sexual health, contraception and in particular condoms. Make sure these are up to date as many young people get bored seeing the same poster in school and youth clubs. Include numbers and information for local family planning clinics. Try and find information about the history of condoms and the use of them by previous generations for the display.

Set up a display of condoms. Try for as wide a variety as possible including colours, flavours and different shapes. If you are not confident about all the different types you could invite a health promotion worker to support the project. Encourage the young people to look at these. Have a selection of free condoms available for those over 16.

During the course of the session make sure that there are plenty of opportunities for the group to ask lots of questions. This can be specifically about the condoms, but could include other discussions such as when it is the right time to start a sexual relationship or whose responsibility contraception should be. Make sure that there are seating areas set up to encourage small discussions and youth workers around to facilitate groups.

Any issues raised can be addressed in further sessions.

71 POSITIVE RELATIONSHIPS

Collage is a fast and fun way of creating a powerful image or message. If you have a large group divide them up so that no more than four young people are working on any one image.

AIM

To look at positive relationships portrayed in the media and begin to question how young people feel who do not fit this profile and where they can find positive role models.

YOU WILL NEED

- Newspapers and magazines (make sure there are plenty that are aimed at the teen market)
- Scissors
- Glue
- Markers
- Large sheets of paper or card
- Blu-tack (to stick the collages up with)

HOW TO DO IT

Working in groups of three or four ask the young people to look through the selection of media images you have collected and produce a collage that represents positive relationships.

Hand out glue, scissors and pens. Suggest that the groups may want to add words to their images by either cutting out letters or slogans from the newspaper, or by using a marker pen.

Allow approximately 30 minutes for the young people to collate their pictures and make the collages. As they finish ask them to stick their work up and encourage the young people to look at what other groups have produced. Ask for a spokesperson from each group to explain the main points and answer any questions.

Bring the group together and use the collages as a discussion starting point. Encourage the young people to consider what images are promoted by the media. Are couples featured who have physical disabilities? How are gay and lesbian relationships shown? How does it feel if you do not match the images shown? Are they realistic? Ask the group to think where people who do not fit the stereotypes promoted can find positive role models that reflect themselves. Identify ways that individuals can challenge inequalities.

72 SHARE/NOT SHARE

This session was developed to use with groups of up to 12 young women, but you could change some of the gender specific cards and use it with young men too.

AIM

This introduces the idea that there are parts of ourselves that we share with different people and bits that we choose to withhold. The aim is for the cards to promote discussion about what is appropriate to share, how we select and how this differs depending on our own comfort zones.

YOU WILL NEED

- 3 x pieces of card headed 'Share with friends', 'Share with partner', 'Keep to self'
- A copy of the 'Share/not share' cards

HOW TO DO IT

Explain to the young women that this is basically a sorting game. There is no wrong or right answer because it is up to the individual to decide what things to share about themselves with others. Suggest that information is shared at different points in relationships, for example, you may choose to share things with a friend that you have known some years but not with new acquaintances.

Place the three headings in front of the group in a line from left to right. Then hand out the 'Share/not share' cards.

Once the group is clear about what is being asked of them make the proviso that if there are any differences of opinion as to which heading a card should go under, the card cannot be placed until discussion has taken place and a compromise agreed. This can take some time if there is a major disagreement, but create space for the debate and encourage the group to see this as a valuable part of the session.

You can facilitate this process by questioning or challenging decisions and ensuring that everyone in the group is being heard and their opinion taken into account.

The game ends when all the cards are sorted.

SHARE/NOT SHARE

My dad's not my real dad	I hate having my hand held	I have my period
I have a criminal record	My mum hits me	I like to be cuddled
I am a virgin	I think I am ugly	I wish my breasts were bigger
I like my hair being touched	I wish I was thinner	I am not on the pill
I don't know how to use condoms	I like clubbing all night	I am being bullied at school
When I go to town I often shoplift	I have been chosen for the hockey team	Sometimes I make myself sick after I've eaten
I think I may be pregnant	That teacher told me I am sexy	I'm not always allowed to go out
I have headlice	I want to leave home	I plan to go to university
I don't fancy boys	I am not sure I believe in God	I borrowed something and lost it
I worry that I am too tall	I am not sure what a French kiss is	I have inherited £5,000

73 ROLE PLAY

As with all drama-based sessions this will lead wherever the young people take it. Often this is dependent on how much they relate to the situation described at the start. The scenarios offered are for single-sex small groupwork, but you can always make up your own to suit the young people you are working with.

AIM

To encourage young people to empathise with a fictional character's circumstance and resolve any issues or conflict.

YOU WILL NEED

- Two chairs pushed together

HOW TO DO IT

Set the scene by explaining what role play is and what you are asking the young people to take part in. Contain the whole exercise by setting a time limit for the activity. This will depend on the size of your group and how keen they are on taking part. You can always negotiate more time with the group if they want it.

Place two chairs in front of the group. Explain that this is now the stage and as you sit here you become the character in the scene.

Ask for two volunteers to come forward. Now read either of the following:

> *You are sitting on a park bench with your best friend discussing your new boyfriends. She shows you a photo of him with her and you realise that it is the same person you have been seeing ...*
>
> *You are sitting on a park bench with your best mate. You thought you saw him kissing your girlfriend as you arrived late at a party last night ...*

Show the two young people to the chairs – these become the park bench. Let them pick up the story from there. When they have run out of things to say or three minutes is up, two more young people go forward and carry on the conversation.

Keep going until everyone has had the opportunity to have his or her say. Be sensitive to anyone who feels uncomfortable taking part in the acting. If you know that you have members who will hate it, try and offer them a non-acting role such as timing the actors to make sure no budding thespian tries to hijack the process!

If the group enjoy role play suggest that they think up another scenario and work through that one too.

74 JEALOUSY BAG

This is thought provoking but good fun! You will need to be sensitive to potential emotions that this may raise to the surface. It can be used with up to 15 young people, but is not as effective in small groups.

AIM

To identify and share things that arouse jealousy and provoke discussion.

YOU WILL NEED

- Post-it notes
- Pens
- An opaque bag

HOW TO DO IT

Ask the group to make a large circle and sit down. Pass around the Post-it notes and a pen to each young person. Ask them to write on their piece of paper one thing that makes them feel jealous. You will need to agree some groundrules on this as the slips will be shared later, although they will remain anonymous.

If the group seem slow to start make a few suggestions. This could be something like 'seeing my boyfriend looking at other girls' or 'my girlfriend's best friend' or 'girls preferring my mate'.

Once everybody has finished, ask him or her to fold the paper so no-one else can see what he or she has written and place in the bag as you pass it around.

Collect the bag and shake it so that the papers get mixed up well. Now pass the bag back around the circle in the opposite direction.

As each person takes the bag they pull out a slip and read the contents. If they pick out their own they should fold it back up and return for someone else.

Leave space for comments or a short discussion after each reading. Are there any duplications or similar themes? Is feeling jealous at some stage a common emotion? Make sure that if identities are guessed the group does not direct their comments at the young person. This is a group process, not an opportunity to work through issues with individuals.

Close the session by agreeing any additional work identified that the group would like to look at in the future.

75 WORD BAG

This is a variation on the previous activity, but is a really good way to introduce potentially controversial issues. Once again to work really effectively participants should remain anonymous so that the words written on the paper slip can be discussed freely.

AIM

To provoke conversation and debate to open a project or discussion group.

YOU WILL NEED

- Small slip of paper for each group member
- Pens
- An opaque bag

HOW TO DO IT

Set chairs in a circle and ask the young people to sit down. Give out a pen and slip of paper to each member of the group.

Tell the young people you are going to call out a word and you would like them to write on their paper what they feel when they hear the word. Explain this can be an emotional response, a question or what they understand by the word. You will need to agree some groundrules on this as the slips will be shared later, although they will remain anonymous.

Choose a word that introduces the project. For example, if this is going to be a project around relationships you could use the word 'heterosexual' or 'lesbian'. What you are looking for is something that will help you establish the existing levels of understanding within the group to base future sessions on.

Once everybody has finished, ask him or her to fold the paper so no-one else can see what has been written and place in the bag as you pass it around.

Collect the bag and shake it so that the papers get mixed up well. Now pass the bag back around the circle in the opposite direction.

As each person takes the bag they pull out a slip and read the contents. If they pick out their own they should fold it back up and return for someone else.

Leave space for comments or a short discussion after each reading. Are there any duplications or similar themes? Is everyone clear what the word means? Challenge any homophobic comments or give additional information if there is any confusion. Make sure that if identities are guessed the group does not direct their comments at the young person. This is a group process, not an opportunity to work through issues with individuals.

You can go through the process as many times as the young people want to - encourage them to choose their own words.

Close the session by agreeing any additional work identified that the group would like to look at in the future.

EVALUATION

76 VIDEO DIARY

This method of evaluation owes much to the fact that so many of us were avidly watching Big Brother last summer! Luckily, it would seem that most young people were too, as I have never needed to give many explanations as to what we are trying to do!

AIM

To allow each young person space to talk to the camera about the activity/session they have just taken part in.

YOU WILL NEED

- A video camera
- Tripod stand for the video camera

HOW TO DO IT

Set up a video booth where the young people can sit quietly away from the rest of the group. All you need is a chair facing the camera on the tripod. It looks better for the replay if you have a blank wall behind the chair or a piece of cloth as a backdrop.

Introduce the evaluation process and explain what you are asking the group to do. Make sure you tell the young people who is going to see the video footage and what you are going to use it for. If you want to play it back to the whole group at a later stage, you will need to get agreement from everyone. They need to be clear what is happening so that they can choose what to say! Additionally you may need to get parent/carer's consent if you plan to show the film to a wider audience.

Invite each young person in turn to enter the booth and speak privately to the camera. This should encourage them to be honest in their responses. This is also a good evaluation method for groups that include young people who are not comfortable reading or writing.

Finally, add your co-worker's and your own comments to the film and you have a complete recording of everyone's account of how the session went!

77 TODAY I ...

A quick and easy evaluation method that needs no preparation! It works with any age and size of group.

AIM

To encourage the young people to focus on one positive experience they have had today during the session.

YOU WILL NEED

- Nothing

HOW TO DO IT

Ask the young people to form a circle facing each other.

In turn ask them to say 'Today I ...' followed by something positive that has happened to them during the session they have just taken part in. This can be factual such as 'Today I learnt something about the law and how it affects me', or a response that focuses on feelings such as 'Today I realised that other people feel the same way as I do when they start a new relationship'.

If someone is struggling to think of what to say, offer the option to pass and return to him or her at the end of the circle. Make sure no-one feels uncomfortable or pressured into make a lengthy response or talk about feelings that have arisen that they don't want to share with the group.

Close the group by offering a 'Today I ...' of your own.

78 FACES

A very simple way to get instant feedback of how a session was received by the young people.

AIM

To find out how the group feels after taking part in your session.

YOU WILL NEED

- A post-it note for each group member
- A good range of pens

HOW TO DO IT

Before the session stick a large piece of coloured paper onto the wall. This will become your evaluation board at the end of the activity.

After you have finished the session hand out a Post-it note to each young person, with a pen.

Ask them to think about how they feel having participated in the session, and then draw a face to represent this on the paper. This should be really simple and show either a smiley, straight or turned down mouth to represent how they feel.

When they have drawn their face ask them to stick the note onto the piece of coloured paper on the wall. Ask the young people to look at all the stickers. Are there mainly happy or sad faces?

Collect them in and use as part of your evaluation for the session.

79 QUICKEST EVALUATION EVER!

This is a particularly effective way to get instant feedback after a session. All young people can take part, including younger members and those who find writing difficult.

AIM

To give workers a fast and basic evaluation of how the young people received the session.

YOU WILL NEED

- Nothing

HOW TO DO IT

Ask the young people to gather together. Ask them questions that you need to evaluate the session. For example: 'Do you feel that you learnt anything new this evening?'

To respond they give one of three signs. Make sure they understand the meanings.

Thumbs up – yes

Thumbs down – no

Thumbs straight – not sure/partly

By counting the numbers of each sign you should be able to see quickly if the session met its objectives. This will inform your planning for the next time you meet.

80 CIRCLE TIME

Circles are good ways to end sessions so that everyone can see each other and nobody feels outside the group.

AIM

To get feedback from each member of the group without interruption from the others.

YOU WILL NEED

- Any small object that can be passed around the group

HOW TO DO IT

Ask the group to form a circle with the youth workers.

Show the group the object that you have chosen. This could be something like a pen, but you could choose something with more significance. I have used a small teddy with younger groups or a ball.

Explain that only the person holding the object can speak. When they have finished they pass it onto the next member of the group.

Ask questions that will evaluate the session. For example: 'What part of this evening did you enjoy most?' 'Name me one thing you learnt tonight.' Make sure you ask the same question of each person to get an overall picture. The number of questions you ask will depend on the size of the group.

Review the answers after the session with your co-worker and record the findings.

81 WORDSEARCH

This is a good way to get young people to reflect on their experiences, but is not too daunting for anyone who is not confident with writing and spelling.

AIM

To encourage each member of the group to reflect on their experience of the session they have just participated in.

YOU WILL NEED

- A copy of the wordsearch for each group member
- Pens

HOW TO DO IT

Hand out copies of the wordsearch and circulate pens.

Ask the young people to look at the wordsearch and choose three words contained in the puzzle that sum up how they felt during the session/activity. If you know that you have a high percentage of young people who find reading and writing difficult, suggest that they do it in pairs.

Collect the information and use to evaluate the young people's experience of the session with your own recordings. Any changes or further work can be developed from this.

Collect in the sheets and evaluate the feedback offered.

WORDSEARCH

Look at the words below. Which ones describe best how you felt during the session that you have just taken part in? When you have decided, find them on the puzzle and put a ring around those words.

Confused, Scared, Informed, Bored, Normal, Lonely, Safe, Comfortable, Shy, Angry, Trust, Assertive, Confident

C	C	A	S	S	E	R	T	I	V	E	C
A	O	U	P	D	Y	L	E	N	O	L	O
F	N	N	O	E	H	R	X	T	P	I	M
J	F	O	F	E	S	T	S	E	K	T	F
L	I	R	I	U	A	D	E	R	O	B	O
P	D	M	Q	A	S	A	F	E	D	S	R
N	E	A	M	A	L	E	A	T	T	D	T
T	N	L	D	S	T	T	D	E	S	A	A
W	T	S	C	A	R	E	D	D	U	O	B
Y	M	J	I	S	U	A	N	G	R	Y	L
I	K	O	H	R	S	T	A	A	T	A	E
C	A	L	N	D	E	M	R	O	F	N	I

82 THANK YOU

This evaluation encourages the young people to think about the role that other group members have played in making the session a success for them.

AIM

To build confidence and appreciation of each other within the group.

YOU WILL NEED

- Pens
- Small Post-it pads

HOW TO DO IT

Ask everyone in the group to reflect on the session that they have just participated in. Encourage them to think who was important to them? Who enabled them to succeed? Who made them laugh? Who supported them?

When they have thought about it ask them to write a positive comment on a Post-it pad and put it on to the back of a group member. Try and facilitate this so that each group member has a note. If you think this may be a problem agree groundrules beforehand so that the group is aware of what is appropriate and what is not.

Review with the group and reflect.

83 HOW I FEEL NOW

This evaluation sheet asks for a very personal view of the session that the young person has just participated in. It only works with small groups that have developed trusting relationships with workers.

AIM

To encourage young people to acknowledge other group member's part in their learning as well as their own.

YOU WILL NEED

- Copies of the assessment sheet
- Pens

HOW TO DO IT

Hand out copies of the sheet and ask the young people to look and think about the statements it contains.

Ask them to reflect on the session they have just experienced and fill in the gaps.

Depending on how well you know the group and the level of confidence the young people have, encourage the group to share their responses. If you do not think that this would be appropriate you can discuss them individually or collect in and review later.

HOW I FEEL NOW

I am pleased ....is here because ....

....

I would like to thank ....because ....

....

I enjoyed doing ....because ....

....

I learnt ....about myself and ....

....about others

I would like to meet with the group again because ....

....

....

My thought for next time is ....

....

84 QUESTIONNAIRE

This is a more traditional form of evaluation that encourages young people to reflect on their experiences. It is also a really good way of assessing how successful an activity has been with a group.

AIM

To record young people's learning outcomes at the end of a session.

YOU WILL NEED

- Copies of the questionnaire
- Pens

HOW TO DO IT

Hand out copies of the questionnaire and a pen to each participant.

Ask them to consider the activity that they have just taken part in and answer the questions on the sheet.

Encourage the young people to share their responses and discuss the session.

Collect the sheets in and review. The comments made will inform any follow-up work or how you structure the session if you plan to run it again with another group.

QUESTIONNAIRE

Name	Date

Please have a look at the questions below and answer as fully as you can.

1 What was the most interesting part of the session you have just taken part in?	2 What part was the least interesting to you?
3 Was the information relevant/useful to you?	4 Have you taken part in similar sessions before? What and where?
5 Did you enjoy the session? Why?	6 What other areas did you expect to be covered?
7 What did you learn?	8 How could you have learnt more?

9 Rate this session from 1 to 10, 1 being poor and 10 being excellent

85 IMAGINE THIS ...

This is another drama-based technique for evaluating how young people feel about the experiences they have just shared. It is suitable for groups of all ages and ability.

AIM

To use a visualisation process to enable young people to assess their own feelings and learning.

YOU WILL NEED

- Candles and matches (optional)
- Music (optional)

HOW TO DO IT

How you create a relaxed, calm environment is up to you and the area you have to work in. One suggestion is to light candles, dim the lights and play music quietly in the background. I have used New Age tapes of the sea and sea creatures to provide a tranquil setting to encourage the young people to relax.

Once you have set the scene ask the young people to either sit or lie down quietly with their eyes closed.

You can use some basic relaxation techniques to focus the group, such as flexing and relaxing limbs and breathing deeply.

As the group begins to chill out ask that they picture a swimming pool on a warm, sunny day. Describe the pool in detail, including a deep end with a diving board and a shallow end with steps. You can be as creative as you want.

Now, suggest that each person use the image of the swimming pool in their head to represent the session they have just taken part in. Where do they see themselves? Struggling in the deep end? Somewhere in the middle? Watching from the side or desperate to dive in? If visualisation is a new experience for the young people use some of these suggestions to get the group thinking on their own. Encourage the sharing of ideas.

Finally, close the session by telling the group to relax and open their eyes gradually as you count to 20.

86 FEELINGS

This is a quick and easy way of finding out how young people feel about the things they have just done. It works with any age, although you need to be sensitive to those with literacy difficulties.

AIM

To get individual feedback from group sessions about how much they enjoyed their time.

YOU WILL NEED

- Copies of the sheet
- Pens

HOW TO DO IT

Give a copy of the 'Feelings' sheet and pen to each young person. Get them to look at the feelings identified and ring those that most reflect how they are feeling at the end of the session. Ask that they do this individually, as it is their feelings that you are interested in. This can be anonymous or named, as they prefer.

Collect in the sheets and use to evaluate the session.

FEELINGS

Trusting Naughty Aggressive

Happy selfish Nervous

left out SILLY tired

SAD cheerful

Unhappy Fired Frustrated

Lonely Proud confident alone

Frightened shy scared loving

Disappointed great peaceful WORRIED

ANGRY safe brilliant

Enthusiastic included trusted

Relieved BORED

embarrassed

87 EVALUATION TREE

This is a creative way of evaluating a session, asking each young person to create a large visual representation of the group experience.

AIM

To build a 'tree' that describes the learning that has taken place in the session.

YOU WILL NEED

- A large piece of paper with a basic drawing of a tree with no leaves on it
- Blu-tack
- Pieces of paper shaped like leaves
- Pens

HOW TO DO IT

Unroll your tree and stick it to the wall or floor with Blu-tack. Introduce it as an evaluation tree.

Hand out a leaf, a pen and a small piece of Blu-tack to each group member. Ask them to think carefully and write on the leaf one word that describes what they have learnt during the session. You can change what you ask for to correspond with what you are trying to evaluate - for example, what did the young people enjoy most? What did they learn?

When they have chosen a word ask the young people to stick their leaf on the evaluation tree.

Review the completed tree with the group and reflect on what has been written.

88 HEADLINES

This is a group evaluation that produces a joint piece of work that depicts the collective experience. As it takes time you may want to use this during the final session of a project. You can use it with any age groups of up to six young people.

AIM

To produce a newspaper front page that shows the group experience of the project they have just taken part in.

YOU WILL NEED

- Newspapers and magazines
- Scissors
- Glue
- Large sheets of paper
- Marker pens

HOW TO DO IT

Hand out paper, glue, scissors and markers to each group of four to six young people. Make available a good selection of magazines and newspapers.

Explain to the groups that the task is to create a newspaper front page of their own that shows what has been learnt/experienced during the project they have been working on.

Suggest that the young people use both marker pens and cut out letters from the newspapers to make the headlines and then devise their copy to go with it. This should include how they feel, what they liked best and anything the groups would like followed up in a further session.

Once the front pages are complete, display them on the wall and invite the young people to review each other's, asking questions or explaining sections as they go along. You can then leave it up as a record of the event for other club members to see.

89 EVALUATION WALL

This provides ongoing feedback of how young people perceive the youth club or project. You can leave it up for set blocks of time before updating it so that the information and comments remain relevant and 'owned' by the young people.

AIM

To encourage ownership of the evaluation process by young people and to make a public record of what is happening in the club.

YOU WILL NEED

- Markers
- A large printed name tag
- Rolls of coloured paper
- String
- Drawing pins

HOW TO DO IT

Identify a wall or area of noticeboard that you can use as your evaluation wall. This will need to be fairly large and agreed with other users of the building.

Cover the area in coloured paper and attach several markers to the edges using the string and drawing pins.

Print off a large tag with the group's name on it and place at the top of the evaluation wall.

Introduce the area to the young people during the next session. Explain that this is their area to write up comments and ideas. You may want to agree groundrules with the group about appropriate language, etc, but make sure you stress that it is up to them what they choose to put there.

You will need to agree how often you are going to update the wall, as information goes out of date quickly and you want the young people to feel an ownership of the process. Inform the club when you intend to change the paper and what you are going to do with the contents.

You can then use this information as part of your evaluation and as a tool to feedback to other young people at members' meetings what suggestions have been made.

90 GIFTS

This evaluation encourages the young people to recognise positive aspects in each other and give it as a gift at the end of the session.

AIM

To promote support and positive regard for group members and raise self-esteem.

YOU WILL NEED

- Small pieces of paper
- Pens
- Opaque bag

HOW TO DO IT

Hand out pieces of paper to each group member. If you have a small group give a piece of paper to each member, if you have a large number of young people hand out one piece only.

Explain that you would like them to write an individual message on their paper for a/each person in the group. Stress that this should be positive, but should include something relating to the session. For example: 'Ruben – thanks for making me laugh' or 'Siobhan – you always listen to everyone's ideas'.

Ask the young people to fold their message unsigned, and write the name of the person they intend to receive the gift on the front.

Collect the gifts and place in the bag. Give it a good shake and then walk among the group distributing the slips of paper. Depending on the young people, they can either look at their gifts within the group or take them away to read later.

Each member of the group should now have some positive feedback about their contribution to the group process.

For information on other resources from the
National Youth Agency, contact
NYA Publications Sales on 0116.285.3709,
e-mail sales@nya.org.uk or fax 0116.285.3777
and ask for a catalogue.

Or, visit the NYA website: www.nya.org.uk

supporting and improving
work with young people

17-23 Albion Street
Leicester
LE1 6GD